EVERYBODY NEEDS HELP

BY PAUL HOBACK SR.

Forward

Several years ago, I was telling Jim Tatum, who is my friend, my doctor, and my Christian brother, that some day I would write a book with testimonies in it, Jim said if I ever did he wanted to write a forward to the book – so I did and so he did and here it is:

I have known Paul for years having met him in Community Bible Study. His demeanor is joyful and evidence of transformation. I enjoyed reading about Paul's journey in life and his call to Christ. He reminds us of God's presence in creation and His revealed word to us in the Bible. The gospel message is outlined by Paul and in the testimony of his friends. I would recommend this book to see how God has changed the life of one of his children.

Introduction/Premise

What is your premise dad? That's what my son asked when I showed him what I was writing. I guess we'll just have to wait and see. It occurred to me after he asked this, and I thought about it, that some people are born blind (not my son but just thinking of where was I going with this?), some people lose their sight to accidents, some lose their sight to physical failures (macular degeneration, glaucoma, detached retinas, etc.) and then there are those of us who just refuse to see or only see the inside of their eyelids, like me. Well maybe a little farther than our eyelids but only as far as we need to see to get us through our daily lives. I know it took me 55 years and God to pry open my eyes and reveal what an absolutely wonderful creation he had made for us to see and participate in.

So – I guess my premise is: look around you and enjoy the life God has given us, not as a bystander, but jump in and take and give as much as you can. When in doubt as to direction, follow our Lord as he has shown us in our Christ Jesus. Most importantly, know that Jesus Christ is our Lord and Savior. Learn all you can about our Lord and love him with all your strength. Give as you would receive. I guess help those who need help and by so doing you will most definitely help yourself and those close to you. There actually is a wonderful guide book already written and tested: the Bible. Read and study it, sup on it, digest it, and make it part of you. You will never regret it - even for eternity.

Index

Chapter 1: Everybody Needs Help

Guess first of all I need a title. Let's see what can I use. Maybe I should write it first then see where that leads and what pops out to us. So let's get started: I was born at an early age – (no that was used before). I lived to a very old age (no that's just wishful thinking). How about: "**Everybody Needs Help**". For my whole life, looking back, I can see where people really needed help. Kids, parents, neighbors, teachers, co-workers, ... everybody. How they got the help and who they got it from varied widely and thus the results they got from that help varied hugely. Some people (especially in my family) got help from chemicals (alcohol, prescriptions, street drugs, etc.). These usually turned out badly. Some people got help from other people (who probably needed help). These turned out well sometimes (I think depending on why the help was given or received). And a number of people got help by turning to our ultimate source of help – our Lord. This, in my experience, usually turns out well.

Now, not everybody needs to receive help. Some people thankfully need to give help (hopefully this will mostly work out evenly). Also most people who need to receive help don't need to receive it all the time. In fact, most people receiving help during their lives also give help to others. Isn't that wonderful? I would guess some people give and receive simultaneously. This is really starting to get complicated, but again wonderfully. How do you manage this and time this? I can only thank our Lord that He somehow controls this, because I am absolutely sure that no combination of governments or individuals could do so very well. We are all individuals with distinct needs and abilities; we are "multisided"

1

beings. To meet the needs of people, all governments seem to try to serve the needs by designing: bureaus, associations, agencies, or whatever. They are created to help a certain size fits all. The fits all size (or "sides") fits nobody and results in people having to accept help that is largely wasteful and wasted.

I grew up mostly in Kentucky and some in Pennsylvania. (Funny how people look at people from Kentucky as being needy and fail to realize that everybody needs help, especially those looking down their noses at others). We didn't have a lot of things but we had a lot of emotional turmoil throughout my growing up. Not all the emotions were pleasant. My dad needed help with his emotions and used alcohol to help him – this definitely did not work. My mother needed help with her children, her environment, and her husband – she used emotional turmoil for help (and later prescription drugs) – this definitely did not work and caused my dad to need more help which caused my mother to need more help which .... well, you know. My mother also asked for and received a lot of help from my grandparents and others (I often think that if you get too much help it becomes a negative help) – if that makes any sense at all - maybe we'll dig more into that later in Chapter 11: Not All Help Helps.

There were 3 children in our family and we all definitely could have used help – spiritual, social, emotional, and probably a lot of other areas. My brother joined the armed forces when he was 17 and got help from the Marine Corps (discipline and self control among other items) – this helped him in some areas but not all, because he began using the same solution for help that our dad had used (alcohol). My sister usually got help from others and asked for help from others – this help did not always address whatever she needed (and probably added to my thoughts that not all help helps). I grew up without a lot of supervision and was mostly a wild child – I needed a lot of help, but never asked and so I never received knowingly.

One source of help for me was an annual extended trip to my grandparents' houses in Pennsylvania. My grandparents always tried to help me even though I did not ask. This first made me aware of unrequited love. The source of this love is, sometimes, from the loving nature of that person, but I believe mostly this love is derived from the love that God so generously pours out on us and we can, in turn, overflow to others. Experiencing this love, in hindsight, definitely helped me. Another experience of this love occurred from a farmer I used to help (from my point of view - from his, I was probably somewhat of a burden). Years later when I was home from college, Mr. Vogt (the farmer's name) called me aside when I was visiting him and asked me why years before I had cut down a row of his corn (with a machete). I remembered doing this, out of anger with my parents, and told him so. He said he thought that something like that was the reason and I needed to get it (the anger) out of my system. He had just watched from a distance and said nothing for those 10 or 15 years! I later thought when he told me this – that is real love (to endure an onerous impact of others on you, in hope they will gain from your loss/outreach). There were lots of other people that impacted my life as a child, but not all helped. Some of these people had, I believe, wrongful intentions of help (helping themselves and not me). I won't go there because I cannot read minds and I do not know what they had in their hearts.

I spent about 4 years in the service (Air Force), 28 years working at a zinc smelter, and another 12 years at a cogeneration power plant. I thankfully found out God had gifted me with an ability to fix things and I made a pretty good living doing so. I'm just sorry I can't say the same thing about my writing abilities. In fact, a majority of my time working was giving help to those who called needing help (with equipment, mostly). The problem with most businesses is they supply only the equipment with help and limit only really addicted people with available help (those who might harm the equipment or people). Only a few really gifted people in authority observed this fact and actually reached out help to those needing help. By this, I mean, psychological counseling, marriage counseling, spiritual guidance and/or a host of other help that is available in today's world. I think a root problem in the military and in business is a conscious effort to divorce our Lord from anything happening in the world; and we are already too separated. The world is a broken place and our only hope is our Lord and Savior – but more on this later.

I met my wife, Sue, in a nightclub and fell in love and we have been together for 42 years so far. I can honestly say we constantly try to help each other. Not always is the help asked for or appreciated, but I think it is offered with love at it's center. Sue is a gifted person in a number of areas. One of those areas is she is a baby whisperer (you know like the "dog whisperer"). She can jump right in, at times of baby distress and take control and calm their distress down. (Too bad this does not work for adults.)

We have raised 2 children (a son and a daughter) and have always tried to help them (again not always was the help asked for or appreciated). I found out the help my mother used and why it was not very helpful (angry emotions) and tried to limit that self help to only a few occasions (I'm sure our children remember fondly each outburst – I was reminded of knocking a hole in the wall once and throwing a fishing pole in frustration – kids have such great memories). My kids were a joy and except for a period of time during their teen years (and possibly a few times in college) were a continuous source of that joy. Both of the kids were very active in school and in after school activities – thank goodness. (Kept them from getting into trouble) Activities kept me from getting into trouble also: at various times I was a den leader, soccer, baseball, football, and basketball coach (and never played any of those things), also with Angela variously involved in track, band, and cheerleading – we never missed any event that I can remember – only God could have figured this out – another thanks to Him. I can remember announcing a wrestling match once (and only once), cause after that I was called Mr. Uhh (I was definitely not a good announcer). I thank God for allowing us to greatly contribute to both the kid's college education so they would not be saddled with a huge amount of debt when they started life on their own (I guess we helped without being asked, but we did it out of love).

I always thought I was a pretty good person, though not at all "religious". But, about 18 years ago, with both kids in college, we were not able to afford to go on vacation. So I looked around for something interesting to do with my vacation time. Not sure how or why, but I began studying weeds (or wild flowers) in the area (my backyard). I ended up collecting over 200 different types and read incessantly about them. (I really had an obsession, I bought a bunch of books, and the whole process took several years). After a lot of time, I found a wonderful interweaving of the plants, animals, funguses, and insects; it sank in: it was ever so apparent that there was a creator behind this awesome display!!! This miniature display is just as impressive in my mind as the heavens displayed every night.

Psalm 19(Bible NIV)

The heavens declare the glory of God;
The skies proclaim the work of His hands.
Day after day they pour forth speech;
night after night they display knowledge.
There is no speech or language where their voice is not heard.
Their voice goes out into all the earth,
their words to the ends of the world.

Then about 12 years ago, I recognized something was missing in my life and I knew I had to do something but I had no idea what. One night I began to pray to God to help me find what I was missing and what I needed to do. In hindsight I was led to:

Romans 8:26

But if we hope for what we do not yet have, we wait for it, patiently. In the same way, the Spirit helps us in our weakness. We do not know what we ought to pray for, but the Spirit himself intercedes for us with groans that words cannot express. And he who searches our hearts knows the mind of the Spirit, because the Spirit intercedes for the saints in accordance with God's will.

Instantly, there appeared in my mind a list (a big list – several pages with small writing) with many items. There is no doubt in me where the list came from or of it's validity. I laughed, because I had thought I was a pretty good guy. The first 2 items on the list were to go to church and to read the Bible. So we did.

As I read the Bible and learned in church (thanks to Henry and Jeff –our pastors at First Presbyterian Church (FPC)), then studied the Bible in CBS (Community Bible Study), thanks to Al Grim and Don and Liz Sullivan, it became apparent, in the wonderfully interwoven and awesomeness of the Bible – that the same creator that was at work in my backyard and in the heavens, had been at work creating the Bible.

I have since learned why the Bible is so important to our learning, and that it most certainly is unerring truth.

Psalm 19:

The law of the Lord is perfect, reviving the soul.
The statutes of the Lord are trustworthy, making wise the simple.
The precepts of the Lord are right, giving joy to the heart
The commands of the Lord are radiant, giving light to the eyes.
The fear of the Lord is pure, enduring forever.
The ordinances of the Lord are sure and altogether righteous.
They are more precious than gold, than much pure gold.
They are sweeter than honey, than honey from the comb.
By them is your servant warned, in keeping them there is great reward.

Then in **Genesis 22**, I learned the love and faith Abraham had in God to be ready to sacrifice his son for Him. Also I learned God's love for us to sacrifice His only begotten son to save us.

Having children I thought of the depth of His love and my hardened heart (I had never realized till then that it was a hardened heart) was torn and melted to realize exactly how much God loves us, knowing our every thought and deed and still loves us. I am forever a follower of Jesus Christ!!!

I have since been led to:

1John 4:7-21

Dear friends, let us love one another, for love comes from God. Everyone who loves has been born of God and knows God. Whoever does not love does not know God, because God is love. This is how God showed his love among us: He sent his one and only Son into the world that we might live through Him. This is love: not that we loved God, but that he loved us and sent his Son as an atoning sacrifice for our sins. Dear friends, since God so loved us, we also ought to love one another. No one has ever seen God; but if we love one another, God lives in us and his love is made complete in us.

I enjoy helping others and God has guided me to share what ever skills I have with others in the hope that by sharing the love that God has poured out on me with others, they will be reminded of His love or learn to hunger to know Him better. FPC has given me the opportunity – through the Fix It Brigade, our Home Repair efforts, and now the Carpenter's CHORE, to do this.

Additionally, in **Genesis 9:1,** that same year, I learned that after God cleansed the world and saved Noah and his family, he instructed them to "be fruitful, increase in number and fill the earth." I think, we, after being cleansed spiritually by the Holy Spirit, have a similar obligation to go forth and be fruitful, increase in number, and fill the earth spiritually, by spreading the Gospel and witnessing to others.

Additionally, also from:

Psalm 19:

Who can discern his errors? Forgive my hidden faults
Keep your servant also from willful sins; may they not rule over me.
Then will I be blameless, innocent of great transgressions.
May the words of my mouth and the meditation of my heart
Be pleasing in your sight, O Lord, my Rock and my Redeemer....

Some time ago, I looked up evangelize in the Webster's New Collegiate Dictionary: to preach the gospel or to convert to Christianity.

When I first became a Christian, God softened my heart and I think I became more caring and observant of others. I had seen many people previously helping others, but had always thought they had some unknown motives. When we joined FPC, Jeff suggested we all get involved in some church works areas.

Sue, being a baby whisperer, volunteered in the nursery, and I volunteered to help Fix It Brigade (this is an outreach effort using Christian people to help handicapped people with problems with their homes) and I also had chances to do visitation with Jim Buck and Chris Rush (two of our deacons). I had a chance then to see true Christian love in action. Jim and Chris absolutely overflow God's love to all they meet and visit and do not hesitate to tell the good news of Christ.

In the Fix It Brigade, Pat Grim lined up work with many needy people and I saw how much she really cared, giving Christ the credit, witnessing to them, overflowing God's love, and how it affected these needy people. Most of these needy people were hurting physically, spiritually, and/or psychologically (they were in bad shape). Just knowing someone cared opened up many of them to receiving the gospel and how much Christ loved them. Lives were changed and, many times, hope appeared. This is real help.

I learned Christ's love is poured out on us greatly. We should not just hoard it, but we should overflow it to others. Love is the only thing I know that the more you give it the more you get. People don't much remember our words but do remember deeds, so Pat taught me to let our work speak lovingly to others. But always, always let them know what Christ has done for them and what the Good News is.

John 3:16

God so loved the world that he gave his only begotten son, that whoever believes in him shall have eternal life. You can't get any more loving than that!!!

THE REAL SPIRIT OF CHRISTMAS

Several years ago while at a store in Rochester, I happened to be watching the Salvation Army kettle and the people passing by it. A young girl wearing a blue coat passed by and paused before going out the outer door. The girl must have walked to the store since she was much too young to drive. She had a small bag of groceries and a small purse. She began digging through her purse and finally bent down and dumped it's entire contents on to the ground. All the while a steady stream of people were passing by. After several long moments the girl refilled her purse and came back to the kettle and put in the coins that she had been so intently digging for. It struck me like a load of bricks that here indeed was a person with the true spirit of Christmas. How fortunate that she has received this spirit so early in her life while some of us take so long to learn or perhaps never do.

This little girl showed she had a need to help. The Salvation Army always has a need for people like her because they have a lot of people in need of help. Her act will always be an inspiration to me.

CHAPTER 2: GROWING UP

My earliest memories are of Richardsville, Kentucky. We lived on a small farm there. (my father was a construction foreman for a large construction company, thus our need to move around a lot. Our family lived, reportedly, before my memory begins, in over 40 states.) My brother had a pet pig and you will never guess it's name (wow, you're right – Porky). My brother rode it to the barn every night and it ate only corn bread and butter milk. Porky got fat fast, and was sold at market when we moved. My most terrifying memory of the farm was the rooster that lived in the back yard. He seemed to have a vendetta against me. Unfortunately the outhouse was in the backyard. I think this was where my bed wetting problem began (lasted till I was about 12 years old). The next, most vivid memory I had was of my mother and dad arguing about his drinking. Little did I know this would continue as long as he lived. We also had a black cat (yep – named Midnight). We had to leave poor Midnight in Richardsville when we moved to Frankfort, Kentucky. This was traumatic to me and really to Midnight. I heard later that he was a real terror in the neighborhood, to every other creature that lived there. We had left him with no help – shame on us.

I only have a few memories of Frankfort: foremost was pushing my sister into a clump of cactus that grew by the front porch. The results definitely hurt me more than her. Another memorable event occurred when my mother was making engraved aluminum trays (using turpentine), and my sister came by and drank the glass of turpentine. There followed a great deal of screaming that ended when my father (with my sister upside down) forced her to throw up the offending chemical. Funny how some helping events imprint on you. One other happening that I can remember was when my father brought home some mammoth and mastodon teeth he had found while building an annex on the governor's mansion. The fossils were donated to the museum at the University of Louisville.

Jump now with me to the west end of Louisville, where I attended Kindergarten. The memories that were embedded there, are of a Christmas play that the kindergarten class put on that included Santa Claus and his reindeer. I was a reindeer and Rudolf was a girl named Leslie. Not sure why this stuck with me but probably the stress of being on stage. Another poignant event was a charity circus that my brother put on to raise donations for Children's Hospital and I was ordered to be a clown (I had no other gifts then). After looking out at the crowd (maybe 6 people) I panicked and began sobbing that I could not go out there (I was in my most colorful PJ's). But the show must go on and I'm sure I entertained the audience with my tears. The only other thing that comes to mind is my brother being very upset with me following him constantly (funny how older siblings-he was 6 years older than I- have a much more interesting life than we do). My brother tired of helping me out by allowing me to follow him and sat on me. I was really happy my mother rescued me, but I think my brother might have resented me even more after that.

Now let's move to where I finished growing up (later I grew in other dimensions). This was to the outskirts of Louisville: Shively. We rented a small house on Likens Avenue. My mind must have improved, because I can remember a lot of stuff here. We again had a few animals (what is it that causes kids to remember animals more than other things in life? My thoughts are that remembering and living around God's creations are much better than remembering and living around manmade creations. Manmade is not as memorable as God's creations simply because man is so broken and passes on this brokenness many times in his creations.) The animals included rabbits, cats, dogs, and goats (the goats were actually the neighbors- more about them later). Each of us kids had a rabbit. We would play with them in the yard after school. They were different colors so we could tell them apart. One day we came home from school and my dad had cooked all three – this is another vivid memory! I found out later from my dad's dad (he was also in construction and always on the road) that once he brought home a puppy for my dad and a few weeks later when he left – his mother directed my dad to take the dog out back and shoot it. She probably needed a lot of help, but so did my dad after that! We all are so broken and easy to break even more, so take care.

I seem to see a repeated cycle here that I should mention – hurtful actions/deeds seem to be reflected in future hurtful actions. (duh) Or even, lack of helpful actions, seem to be reflected in future lack of helpful actions.

I have to add a paragraph or two here about the dark time of my life, not to make you feel sorry for me but because I got through it and have not dwelled on it or used it as a crutch. Begin with me in second grade when I had infected tonsils and adenoids, so bad in fact I could hardly hear. I had to sit by the teacher's desk in order to hear her (this was like full time playing a clown as in the above circus). The offending body parts were removed later in the year and the suggested benefit of unlimited ice cream was never fulfilled (I threw up blood for several days and could eat nothing). During the period of second grade through about 7th or 8th grade my teeth rotted out. I was in pain most of the time, hot water bottles and aspirin were my only friends. This finally ended when my mother finally took me to a dentist and fillings and extractions took place. But the worst events that impacted my life were the screaming and arguing between my parents. It was incessant. On many occasions, I rolled in a ball in the back seat of the car and prayed to anyone out there to stop them. This finally happened when we were traveling to my grandparent's house in Pennsylvania. We were going through Cincinnati, Ohio, in the early morning hours. My dad (driving) was, as usual, drunk, and my mother was screaming at him. They were hitting at each other as we traveled (this seems unsafe to me now and really it was). My brother, who was about 16 at this time, finally punched my dad senseless or maybe into sense. The fighting, along with the car, stopped in a bad section of town, police were called and my memory next jumps to arriving in Pennsylvania. The marriage between my mother and dad ended soon after that.

During this period, my father had a great job and earned a pretty good living. However, towards the end he would disappear on Fridays after being paid and then show up on Sunday with no money. The addicted totally worship the chemical (such as alcohol) and will do anything to follow where it leads. Our family was fed by an old Biblical principle: gleaning. We would pick up bottles in ditches in the area. You could take them to a grocery store and get two cents apiece for them. Hard to think of that situation now, but never felt terribly burdened by this as we lived through it.

The next dark time follows in my mother working 7 days a week 12 hours per day (as an LPN, licensed practical nurse). She was hardly ever home and we had a scary looking (witch-like) sitter looking after us. She was from the family next door who owned the goats, actually the middle child (30's). She was truly a broken person who suffered from many things including epilepsy. She, sometimes, fell into an unconscious state and we would have to call her older brother next door to assist her, which involved rubbing an onion on her face. Her employment ended soon after she chased my sister and I through our house with a butcher knife (I locked myself in the bathroom, refused to open the door for my sister, and so she hid under a bed). I think my sister shared more information with my mother than I did, because I would never tell my mother unhappy information, but somehow our baby sitter was let go (whew!). Her younger brother (20's) is also a dark memory of mine. He pursued my friends and I around the area, trying to fondle us. This finally ended when he followed me around our home and I had to get our trusty butcher knife and threaten to kill him if he did not leave me alone. I was only about 10 at the time and it was very scary. He left me alone after this. A few months later he was arrested about a mile away for molesting a boy and I never saw him again.

My mother remarried a much older guy who was pretty emotionless to us all (we didn't get along too well, I got beat a few times- razor straps hurt – my fault- he was the adult), but he did say hurtful things to me like: I would never amount to anything and several times "you have a mind of your own" –I was kind of proud of that one for many years. I had a lot of fear of my step father and used to keep a knife under my pillow for a lot of the time during this period.

Another problem I had in this dark period was my vision: I needed glasses. I could hardly wait for my mother to go to bed at night so I could put her glasses on and properly see television (yes we had finally gotten our own TV.) My mother finally took me to an eye doctor and I got glasses. Glasses for a child are a real challenge and led to a lot of consternation when at various times I broke them, in every conceivable manner.

A note here, about the darkness, that we encounter throughout our walk in this world. You often wonder why God allows this darkness (suffering) to exist. It is a broken world and he has done the ultimate to heal it – sent us his only begotten son. God, I think, allows darkness to exist (I'm sure he could end it at anytime, but to man's detriment- in separating the wheat from the weeds too early, some of the wheat would be lost). There are other reasons for this darkness. It is the result of this broken world; however, it can make us stronger or improve our faith or insight. It is there to allow God to glorify himself by showing his light. It is there to break the hardened hearts that some of us have and by so doing bring us into His light. And I'm sure there are other reasons, but who can know the mind of God (or council him)? I can only trust in him and try to follow as he calls.

I can honestly say I forgive everyone who was in this dark period of my life (my parents, my neighbors, my step father, everyone). However, if the right person was in the right place to help me and had the where-withal to help, a lot of pain could have been avoided. I read a wonderful book a couple of years ago I would suggest to everyone: "The Shack" written by William P. Young. It is a little bit strange but the point of the book, I think, is the epitome of forgiveness (sometimes you have to exaggerate a point to get it across, don't you think?)

A meditation I learned many years ago was a great help to me. In a quiet place try visualizing yourself when you were a small child in fear and in need of help. Now, visualize going back in time to that hurting child and hugging him/her, and telling him/her everything will be alright and that you will always be there for him/her. That you love him/her forever and ever and that the hurting he is suffering will soon be over. The child you are helping is inside you and needs your help. Help him/her and you will most definitely help yourself.

Another meditation I learned during this period was to help me with the nightmares that occurred seemingly every night. Nightmares of falling, being chased or just the ground crumbling under me. The end of these nightmares happened after I spent a long quiet time going further and further into myself asking myself why I feared the object of fear in my nightmare(s). After untold levels of asking and answering those questions plus completely recognizing and accepting the fact that the nightmares were sourced completely within me and should be able to be controlled by me (I owned them). They just disappeared and haven't returned since (maybe 55 years now).

I do remember some good events too – my mother and dad volunteered at a local polio clinic (there was a terrible epidemic during the early '50s. They got along well during this period. (my mother was an LPN and my father was a medic in the Navy during WW2). Maybe we humans are built to need to be helpful and working.

We lived on Likens Avenue for the rest of my childhood. Mostly, I have happy memories of this life. But many tragic things did occur: my mother and dad got divorced (though this was better than all that fighting), my father got a ride in an ambulance when he tried to punch a glass door (just prior to the divorce), my father died (after both were remarried – not sure if it was accidental as judged), I spent most of my time roaming the local forests and farms. We stopped attending church after we moved from the west end of Louisville, not sure why but the turmoil of my parents lives probably interfered with their hearing God's voice.

I can remember doing many odd jobs when I was a kid: mowing grass, selling eggs, picking beans, strawberries, tomatoes, and other farm jobs (couldn't shovel snow – not much of that in Louisville). I didn't make a lot of money, but enough to pay for comic books, books, a few hamburgers, and milk shakes. I never had a lot of stuff and didn't really miss what I didn't have. I felt loved by my mother and grandparents, so what else really mattered? I read a lot during these years (escape/ scifi novels mostly – even under my covers at night, when I was supposed to be sleeping – maybe why my eyes went bad?) Again, a lot of my fond memories involved animals: I had a couple of beagle hounds that adopted me and so I spent a lot of time rabbit hunting. I can also remember a pack of dogs from the neighborhood following me (like I used to follow my brother). We (the dogs and I) caught a lot of possums in the woods and brought them home a few times and put a collar and leash on them, you really get some odd looks from neighbors when you walk a possum around the neighborhood. I can remember swimming and fishing in a nearby farm pond. Once, my sister went with me and my mother drove to the pond and caught us swimming – will always remember the limb she pulled off a tree and smacked me with. (a note here to kids: make sure when you ask for permission to do something, your parents really hear you, cause sometimes they are not paying attention). Not sure if this event helped me, but it sure did imprint on me both physically and mentally.

The last couple of years in high school I did participate in track, cross country and high jumping. I did not subject myself too well to practice, so did not get to be great. However, since I had spent many years running around the forests, I could run long distances well. We did (our team) make it to become one of the top teams in the state meet. I had no money, no car, and no social graces so I never got involved in a social life in high school. I did finally find one of my gifts, however, math. I did very well on tests and was mentored by a wonderful math teacher (named Mrs. Owings). I was given a scholarship for $500 – enough for the first year in college and went to the University of Kentucky. (I would like to make note of the fact that I did not deserve this scholarship since my grades in school did not show the discipline necessary to study at college levels). I did get some additional help from my brother. He had me out to his house the 2 summers around my senior year. (to Lincoln, Nebraska and to Columbus, Mississippi. I didn't earn a lot of money but met a lot of nice people and avoided my step father). After my first year in college, I got a job at Wheeling Steel Company and made enough money to pay for another year of college. I must confess here that I largely wasted my time in college. I did a lot of social exploration (partying) and seemed to avoid going to class (not sure why). This definitely is not conducive to staying in school. So, next I jump to beginning an apprenticeship at St. Joe Zinc Smelter in Monaca, Pennsylvania.

For the rest of my life I never goofed off again and have since gotten top grades in everything. Sometimes you have to fail, without help, to change your character to doing good. The timing of giving and receiving help is of utmost importance. So, I guess you can say withholding help sometimes is the best help.

I do remember having a number of emotional events when my sister and mother had some dramatic conflicts. I was upset with my sister and her husband for many years after this. I do feel she repents the problems that arose. I know I have forgiven all the conflicts, and I know absolutely where my mother is, that there are no hard feelings. Again, we must all reach a point of forgiving all people their trespasses as we would have our Lord forgive our trespasses. (this sounds familiar, huh?)

I worked at the Zinc Smelter for about 3 months before fear of being drafted (remember Viet Nam) motivated me to join the Air Force. I was selected to join the Air Force Security Service and attended training in Biloxi, Mississippi as an intercept operator. We were "listeners". I spent 2 years in Anchorage, Alaska and one year in Udorn, Thailand. I was very good at my job and greatly enjoyed it, but not military life. I think you have to be somebody special to spend a life in the service. I did meet a lot of wonderful people in the service and they have annual reunions, (unfortunately I cannot always make our reunions), but I keep up with the communications about the reunions. There is something amazing to be included in on what is going on in the world (before the news media even knows).

Let me just say flat out: I did many things throughout my life that were not good or a help to anyone, even myself, they were even sinful. I grew up as a member of the baby boomer generation but really think the name should have been the if-it-feels-good-do-it generation. The real wonder of our Lord and Savior is his willingness and ability to forgive us all the wrongness in our lives. I won't dwell on this wrongness. It's not the reason for this book. God has washed away the guilt and made me a new person. I still have parts of me that require ongoing pruning as in, John 15, Christ tells us we need pruned to remain part of His vine. At CBS the other day, our leader, Don, came up with a quote I really like. It is about someone who approached the great artist Michelangelo who was sculpting a horse out of marble and the person asked him how he can do this so beautifully? He told the man "it is easy – you just knock off what ever does not look like a horse." That is what Jesus is doing to all of us – just knocking off what doesn't look like Jesus. We are all just works in progress.

When I got out of the service I returned to the zinc smelter and finished my apprenticeship as an Instrument Repairman. Before I finished the apprenticeship I began training as an Instrument Engineer and completed this education the year after the apprenticeship. I was put in charge of the Instrumentation group the year after this and worked there until the plant shut down in 1979.

The plant next door called me and offered me a job a couple of weeks after the zinc plant closed. So, I worked there, as an instrument engineer/leader, for 9 months until the zinc plant restarted and they offered me a higher job and with more pay, so I returned there. I was to be the Assistant Superintendent of the power plant (a 125 megawatt coal fired power plant). I spent the next 17 years there learning all about power plants.

After the zinc company was taken over and the new company seemed to not care enough about their people, I put in an application to the cogeneration power plant next door to the zinc company, as a power engineer. I started work there in 1997. The power plant was a wonderful experience in the beginning. It seemed to be a compassionate thinking company that actually adhered to all their people to have fun working, be socially responsible, and other great goals. They actually ran their immense business doing all the fore mentioned. They were in many countries and tried to help those countries advance by offering the people affordable power. It was exciting to travel to some of the places they were developing and participate in the growth. The down fall occurred when the economy fell and some people who made decisions did not do enough homework. Finances tightened up, new management and management techniques were put in place and the fun began to end. I retired as vice president, soon after, in 2009 and began my life's work – Carpenter's CHORE (more on this later). I do more physical work now, but the stress is less and the pay is amazing (0$ now but great fortune in the next life). I am blessed every day. God has helped me during each step of my life but I could not see the help until I looked back from a distance. Try it with your own life and memories.

Alcoholism definitely runs in both sides of my family. My dad, brother, aunts, uncles, cousins, so many other people have had this problem. I have had a touch, of the problem, with alcoholism, but overcame it, probably only due to fear of becoming like them (that and being threatened by my mother and wife if I did). I have always noted this problem to my kids (they may have this genetic predisposition) and I pray that they never will develop this problem.

All the history thus far was what I lived through, now a little history related to me by others: My dad was raised in Racine Ohio, a small town where his great grandparents settled when they ran away from the South during the Civil war. They hooked up with the Northern General Lichter and his army in retreat, plus a bunch of runaway slaves and crossed the Ohio River at Racine Ohio. My dad's great grandmother went into labor and had my dad's grandfather not far from the shoreline, so they stopped there. They remained in Racine until around the 1890's when they traveled to Oklahoma to take part in the Land Rush that was put on there. It did not go well for them there, so they returned to Racine.

My dad's dad and uncle were very active in Rust Engineering and Construction Co. and spent a lot of time on the roads doing various construction projects. A very large project was the construction of the facility in Tennessee (Oakridge) that was used to construct the first atomic bomb. My grandfather said he was not told what he was building but used over 700 pipefitters and 700 carpenters to build it. My dad just stayed in the family business and worked for Rust also. He worked on a project building a smoke stack in Langloth, Pennsylvania where he met my mother and married her in 1938. My dad's family came to America in the early 1800's from Germany (actually left from a port in Poland I understand). They entered America through Philadelphia, Pennsylvania. One of the Hobacks left the area and went out west and was a fur trapper (I believe he was one of the first white men in the West (Wyoming area). A number of mountain, valley, river, etc. are named after him. The rest settled in Virginia. Many reside there until this day (around the Wytheville area).

My mother's family came to America during the middle 18th century from Scotland/Ireland. They came to Burgettstown, Pennsylvania around that time and settled the then frontier. One of their relatives (Finley Scott) settled in the now named Finleyville, Pennsylvania area. My mother's grandmother married a man named William Malone. The marriage was begun under stress because they came from different social strata. But, they had a very long marriage and were a good Christian family. William's father (Carson) was a civil war veteran and lived to be about the last living Civil War veteran in Pennsylvania. A great story of him was told to me by my uncle Deb – when William was just married, Carson gave him his old rifle, and power horn, that he had carried through the civil war, and told him "to keep it clean and ready to use or he would take it back". About a half century later Carson was visiting William and said "where is the rifle he had given him?" William sent Deb upstairs to fetch it. Carson looked down the barrel and said "it's dirty, I'm taking it back." He later gave it to another son. People meant what they said in those days I guess. My son has the powder horn, it was constructed in 1771, according to the date carved in it.

I have many memories of my great grandparents (Malone). My grandmother Malone was a wonderful woman who was a kind of legend during the depression for giving food to hobo's in the area. Somehow they had her house marked as a person who gives help to those who were hungry. My grandmother was a wonderful cook that, I can remember her, baking cookies, chicken and dumplings and many other scrumptious foodstuff. I fondly recall cleaning up cookie dough and cake batter but found out that not all uncooked dough is good. This happened when she had some pancake batter left over and I mistakenly identified it as cake batter (yuck). She always warned me I would get worms from eating this stuff. (a little white lie meant to help me remember I think). Another memory of her was the work she asked me to do – weeding her flower gardens. I really did not enjoy this task but she gave me a little money and I first found out from her the joy of the experience of completing a job (what a help this is to me to this day – just think of the people who never get to experience this joy at an early enough age to help drive them to a productive life!!).

My memory of my grandfather Malone (Bap), his name was originated by my mother's inability to say Pap, is summed up with one summer eating a fresh peach. Bap had me plant the seed in his back yard. The next summer when I returned, there stood a 7 foot peach tree, I was in awe. Years later my uncle Deb related the story of Bap forcing him to go to the local nursery and buy and plant a peach tree in his backyard..... This act of love will always stick with me, and what a help it is. Another event I recall of Bap was when he came up to me when he was nearly ninety and gave me a $20 bill and said "don't tell anyone about this gift, because he couldn't afford to do this for everyone." What an impact/help to know you are specially loved by someone (middle children do have an extra burden to get over).

Thinking back about my great grandparents, they were loving, joyful, peaceful, patient, kind, good, faithful, gentle, and self controlled. Does this sound familiar? All the fruits of the Holy Spirit as in Galatians 5:22. My great grandfather always had his Bible with him (maybe not reading but just holding – he was getting pretty old). This is the way I will always remember them. I think maybe this is the seed that God grew in me, after all, and I have seen this so much in my life- **one's actions are remembered much more than one's words.**

My mother's mother Edna married a man named Harry Parks (a big hero of World War I –many medals including the French Medal of Honor). My grandmother was pretty young when she married Harry and they only had one child – my mother. Harry deserted his family when times got tough, so my mother never knew her dad. The day she graduated from High School, she got a note from her dad saying that he had watched her graduation and apologized for never being there for her. My grandmother remarried a few years later (after Harry left) to a man named Jack Finney. He had psychological problems and spent the majority of his life in a mental institution (Torrance). They traveled many places (even as far as Kansas) looking for a job to support their kids as they had 3 children plus my mother. My grandmother and her children had a tough life, especially during the Great Depression, making it, but got a lot of help from her parents. My grandmother finally got a job with the post office and worked there for over 35 years. (she had never- ending praise for FDR for her job) Times were much easier after that, and I can say she never stopped helping other people (all of her kids and a lot of grandkids plus many others). Again, isn't it great how we can all be receivers and givers of help. She was always ready to give all credit to our Lord.

Looking back at my ancestors, and the challenges they all met and dealt with, what comes to mind is first:

Genesis 26:24

And the Lord appeared to him the same night and said "I am the God of your father Abraham; do not fear, for I am with you. I will bless you and multiply your descendants for My servant Abraham's sake."

19

And then:

Psalm 23:4

Yea, though I walk through the valley of the shadow of death
I will fear no evil;
For you are with me;
Your rod and Your staff, they comfort me.

Do not fear just follow where ever our Lord's calls, where he calls us
He gifts and protects us.

Chapter 3: Working and Child Rearing

We had our oldest child in 1971. Angela was the beginning of our family and our life's education. You really can't appreciate help until you raise a child. You feel so helpless (and you are) especially during times when they are sick. I think one of the finest organizations around now is MOPS (Mothers of Pre-Schoolers). My daughter was very active in this organization while her kids were young. Sure wish we knew they existed while we raised our kids. Angela was pretty healthy actually, after we solved her colic problem (she seemed to be allergic to milk and we switched her to Neo Mulsoy – a soy based food.)

The only thing that makes raising children survivable is being married to a loving partner in all things. Being best friends with your life mate makes all the trials and tribulations seem like just another bump in the road of life and not an insurmountable road block. Sue and I have always been partners in all we do and have. Now, we have not always agreed on things because we are certainly different people with different opinions but when we have worked together and been patient enough to work to reach agreement it has always been a success. I think it is desirable to present a united front to children when you are raising them. Otherwise they (the disagreements) can, indeed, tear a relationship apart.

If we face problems in a loving relationship our Lord will present us with a solution. Knowing what I now know, if we face problems in a loving relationship that is founded in a loving relationship with Christ they (the problems) are an order of magnitude less. I know we, as individuals, must accept Christ as our Lord, but in addition, we as married couples also need to accept Christ, together, as our Lord and Savior. As individuals, for our eternal salvation; and as a couple for our marriage salvation.

Not sure how, but Sue is my biggest fan and my biggest critic. Everyone needs someone to keep them grounded and she does that for me. She was most definitely the main carrier of the child rearing duties. You can tell how well she did by the success of our kids. They are honest loving people and that is due to the constant loving manner their mother put towards this purpose.

We, in child rearing, had our differences though. Sue mostly believed everything they told her. Me, being more worldly-wise, in the manner of a well known TV judge, thought if a teen ager's lips are moving they are lying. Thank God she was in charge.

Another area of disagreement is in my talent for music. She is gifted in this area and seems to know that I have no ability to distinguish between tones, or whether a note is flat or sharp. I, however, concentrate on making joyful noises. (our differences are like looking at a forest – I see the trees and she sees the forest – or maybe I see the birds in trees and she sees the trees and forest??) Yet another point of friction is she thinks she can read my mind! I tell her frequently she cannot. However, she is right very often, not always, but often(….oops don't let her know she is right often). All this included, we have a great relationship even though as pointed out by dear friends, we are like the old radio show "The Bickersons", but then so were these old friends and they have been married far longer than us, so there is hope for all in this.

I will always remember Angela's second birthday, walking into the living room with a piece of cake and ice cream – and then dropping it off her plate – her whole demeanor traveled to the floor with her cake. Happily, her mother got her another and things were fine again. Another flash back is Angela traveling very fast on a plastic elephant toy vehicle and crashing into a tree – our first stitches!!

I worked a lot during our kids early years – our plant worked 6 days plus per week, plus I never refused overtime. We were trying to save enough money to buy a house and pay all our bills (there were a lot since my health insurance didn't pay for Angela's delivery) and wedding rings were paid for over several years. We never did save enough to buy a house but, looking back God worked through my grandmother as she sent a check with enough money to provide a down payment on a house, we did not ask for this help but God knew we needed it. All praise to our Lord, when a really tough bill came in, somehow we came into extra money to pay it (little did I realize our Lord was with us- even then). Then we had our second child, Paul. The insurance paid for his delivery and not a lot of colic but he did get pneumonia and spent a week in the hospital. We definitely needed help during this period – thank God for my In Laws.

My mother passed away just prior to Angela's second birthday, and I deeply regret not telling her how much I loved her, despite knowing her faults and short comings she was still a great and loving mother. I know my sister now feels the same way. A very important lesson here in hindsight: never wait to tell people how you feel about them. This could be the greatest help you can give to others. Christ told us throughout his life how much he loved us and showed this in his ultimate sacrifice. Remember.

As I mentioned earlier, Angela and Paul were always ready to take on new adventures and activities. We took them on vacations everywhere and I think they always had a great time. Trips are a wonderful way to broaden people's world view and minds. I fondly remember the kids in the back seat putting on a radio show, a talk show. They were actually pretty good – as long as neither violated the no-trespass-on-my-side rule.

Angela during various years: was in the girl scouts, high school band (clarinet), track and field, cheerleading, an emcee in a talent show, in the gifted program (which did a lot of neat stuff like put in suggestions for new game packages – she actually got her name on 2 of the cards in a game that was sold for about $40 at "a local toy store near you"). Paul was also very active: early in cub scouts, band (trumpet), soccer, base-ball, basketball, football, and also in the gifted program. Paul seemed to stick with some of his activities to a point he got pretty good at them – especially baseball and football. He played a couple of years of football in college and was offered scholarships in both baseball and football. Paul also had opportunities to try out for a couple of professional base-ball teams. But (after he transferred to Geneva College from Grove City) he told both baseball and football coaches at Geneva that he was going to concentrate only on studying and no sports. Angela finished college with a BS in Nursing and Paul finished college with a BS in Mechanical Engineering. I was very happy to see both with tools to thence earn a living. Both the kids were very independent and rarely asked for help, but as you parents know, we were always ready to offer and give help (especially advice).

In hindsight again, I can see God helping them throughout their jour-ney by putting influential people in their paths. You would have to ask them who were really special but I have quite a number in mind, especially in the areas that we did not do too well. I was not yet a Christian and really, really regret not being able to give them more spiritual guidance. As a parent I definitely failed there. God, however, waits for no man and provided the doorways for them to access Him. Both of my children are Christians – thank you my Lord and Savior.

Chapter 4: God's Creations Speak to Us

As I discussed in Chapter 1, I first learned to see when I was 55 years old. It is also worth noting here-during this time of revelation I spent a lot of time on my knees digging. God called to me through an obsession to learn about weeds (wild flowers). I became fascinated with weeds and all things growing in our neighboring fields, forests, and ditches. I collected and transplanted over 230 different plants. Everything from ginseng to dandelions to skullcap to cardinal flowers were adopted. They were not only beautiful, but fascinating in their needs to flourish. There were even plants that lived on other plants; indian pipes are a plant without chlorophyll and live on the dying parts of other plants. Another is dotter. It is a true parasite that vines over other plants and takes nourishment off of them. Insects were the next to come to light to me. Many separate insects only live, eat, and breed on a certain type of plant. Then came fungi. They and their close relative lichens, are absolutely beautiful to view. When you view all this life along with the many small animals and reptiles that live in wonderful harmony with them, you can truly grasp how there is a Godly interweaving present, even in a small fractal such as our backyard.

When one looks into the heavens, you can see stars, planets, meteors, satellites, comets, and many other things. Scientists can sense many other things such as black holes, neutron stars, dark matter, and galaxies far away, but going up forever. Looking down there are atoms made up of neutrons, protons, electrons and these are made up of quarks, leptons, bosons down forever, even to the Higgs boson (the God Particle) and maybe even gravitons, hadrons and baryons. You can just sense these are all a Godly interweaving in a near infinite manner.

Tearing apart the way the universe works, say in chemistry, physics, electronics, computer logic, and math, you can see a similar Godly interweaving present in ALL things. A recent theory about the structure of all matter uses string theory, theory that all the universe is made up of strings and tied to each other at intersecting points (wow- if that's not interweaving what is).

And finally – last but not least – look at the printed book God has given us – the Bible. You cannot seriously study it without seeing the prophesying in the Old Testament point over and over again to Christ. And see the crescendo of the New Testament in Jesus' life, death, and rebirth, and then the lengthy time and times following his glorification. Such a Godly interweaving cannot possibly be ignored.

When you view all this interweaving you must see the work of the same hand in all things. There is no doubt in my mind or heart that God exists and shouts to us through his creations. Just look, listen, or think. He loves you so much He gave you all three of these senses. He only wants to help us see Him, knowing full well to see Him will lead to us loving and following Him.

I have already noted how God called to me from His creation and, in the first chapter, how He called me to faith by accepting Christ as my Lord. The Bible is so wonderfully written over a period of thousands of years and it has been verified by so many people that you really must accept the divinity of the words in it. God exists and Christ was sent and is and always was God, after He rose to heaven He sent His Holy Spirit to guide us and teach us. His Holy Spirit is with me and you (if you accept Christ as your Lord and Savior). The Holy Spirit is God. I have no idea how all this works, but I know it is truth.

I will in the next chapter relate to you where he has led me since giving me salvation and faith.

Chapter 5: Eyes Opened, another Calling

As I learned of God's love for me, my heart melted. I was called to accept Christ as my Lord and Savior. I think too often people accept Christ as savior but leave out the Lord part. We are called to serve Him as He is our Lord. The other part of the Good News is that He will give us gifts to accomplish His calling. Another blessing I had was the presence in my life of good ministers. Our pastor Jeff advised us to become involved in some part of church work. I got involved in something called the Fix It Brigade. We would, once a month, visit an unfortunate person (aged, widow, or handicapped person) and help them with their house and/or yard. This work would usually take a few hours for me (but not for Al and Pat Grim – the leaders of this mission – they would spend many hours). I did this for a number of years and learned a lot about Christ's love and how it is poured out on us and that we should overflow it to others along with comforting them and reminding them that God has not forgotten them. We began going to First Presbyterian Church of Beaver in March of 2001 and I was baptized in the park in Beaver in July, 2001. Wow, God sure doesn't mess around does he?

A church effort I was blessed to get involved with was being a deacon. Our mission was to take care of church members (especially those who might be having difficulties). I think the aged have a tough time getting by, especially if their families forget them. They, many times, can't get to church and thence can get into a drifting situation. They are limited on how much they can do around their houses and really do need help. We tried to supply them with help by fixing things or even sometimes just visiting with them, this was the Home Repair Effort. Listening to them was a big help. Praying with them was an even bigger help. I even had the feeling, numerous times, that some of the older members of congregation that asked for help, only asked for help to help us, that is, to help us grow in the brotherhood of Christianity, if that makes any sense to you. I know it has since made a lot of sense to me. I spent 3 years in this task.

Everyone needs help at some time in their lives; churches have a better way of seeing and acting on their needs than anyone else. Churches can address the needs that people have, because they know the people in their congregation and have a history with them. We also have a kindred spirit (the Holy Spirit). When you know people and their history, they have a hard time being dishonest with you and trust is built up between you and them. In all, it is just a better way to address help to people.

In addition, when a person needs to share communications with others, who better than a brother or sister in Christ to listen or talk. What a relief to someone stuck in a house (or a home) to sit with somebody who really cares for them.

We, after a while, integrated the Fix It Brigade program with the Home Repair Effort for the congregation, since it was the same people doing the work. The purposes, though, were different. In the Fix It, our purpose was to evangelize and witness to people not in our church. In the Home Repair Effort, our purpose was to comfort those people who were hurting (aged, widows, handicapped, etc.). Regardless of purpose, I was truly blessed for having been involved in both programs; plus meeting so many God fearing people.

Another wonderful learning experience I have had was the opportunity to take part in CLI (Christian Leadership Institute). Our pastor, Henry, was the leader in this training. During the training, we had a wide ranging education on Christian history and how it has and is being used for our salvation and for other Godly purposes. The purpose I had in taking this training was to help me become more confident in my efforts at Christian outreach in our domestic mission programs (Fix It, Carpenter's CHORE, and others). A side benefit, I never predicted, was spending a lot of time with a lot of wonderful people and hearing of their experiences with Christ. Education is so much fuller with a number of people learning in conjunction with us. This experience gives us a great multisided learning opportunity. The Holy Spirit definitely communicates with all Christians, but not the same information – sharing with each other broadens and deepens our experience, plus truly makes us appreciate having so many brothers and sisters. In addition, when the Holy Spirit does communicate the same information to several of us, it exhibits very overtly the kindredness of our Christianity.

A very important gateway, I was allowed to reach, is being able to read and study the Bible. After I did as I was directed and read the Bible, I learned enough to understand I needed help to study it. I really knew I had to get into a Bible study group but could not seem to get into one. I was lamenting this fact to Al Grim (Fix It Brigade) and he introduced us to Don and Liz Sullivan. Between them all, we were invited and joined Community Bible Study (CBS) in September, 2001. We have been with CBS since (11 years now). It is a wonderful organization made up of good Christian people. We have learned so much, and have grown and shared along with all the men and women who are members of this organization. CBS is a world-wide Bible study, non denominational, and has groups in most areas of the USA. We pick a book (or more) from the Bible each year and go over it verse by verse. It is awesome to see how the Holy Spirit brings to light the lives of each of the people in the various classes, and how Christ has worked in their lives.

For the last 6 years I have had the opportunity to serve as an elder in our church. Elders are responsible for the operation of the church. There are 15 elders and the various ministers. We meet monthly and make decisions as to how the church operates, guiding direction and the hows and wherefores of the church. It is extremely important that these men and women are God-fearing people and are led by the Holy Spirit; and also that they be respected in the general community. It does not take too many lost people in a church to lose a church. There are dying churches all over the USA and even in our neighborhood of Beaver County. This is so sad. Just a thought that maybe our Lord prunes not only people but churches as well; that is if a church does not produce the fruit it should, it is pruned in order that more sustenance is given to the branches that are producing fruit.

During the 6 years I have been an elder, we have faced many tough decisions and prayed for many hours for God's help in making the decisions that we were tasked with. The 2 really tough hurdles we faced and decided on, in my estimation, were to leave our old affiliation and join the Evangelical Presbyterian Church, this is not to say we at FPC changed, because I really know in my heart, that our old affiliation changed and left us outside their church. The scripture is God's word and it does not change. We should and will follow God's word.

The outside world will see, Christian churches, as going one of two ways: practicing what is written or practice what is currently culturally attractive. That is to say, I believe, our old affiliation began compromising the word of God and our traditional catechism/confessions to match what many in the world now believed. These beliefs included many ways to salvation, changed definitive rules for clergy or church leadership, and other changes. Our views were that scripture is the word of God and does not change. Our Lord is eternally consistent. Now, we are all sinners and Christians should do all we can do to not judge others, but we have been chosen to travel a difficult path and I personally will not stop my action of following my Lord.

Let me take a little aside here and talk about 2 types of decision-making, conviction and convincing. My fellow elders and I prayed and discussed the idea of leaving our old affiliation for hundreds of hours trying to be convinced one way or the other. I know in my heart the convincing never reached an end and that God convicted us (or at least me) of our path in the final decision. God had to convict me of His existence, then of His path for my salvation, and then for my service to Him. Sometimes convincing is not an alternative. The ways of God are not the same as the ways of the world. Some decisions are beyond us broken humans to make. There are, oh, so many Bible verses to use for guidance for both directions and add to this our natural inclination to stand and fight, but in the end, the decision, I believe, was caused by conviction. I know each of the times God gave me conviction as a doorway, and I took that path, it was the best decision for me. I also know that for 55 years various people tried to convince me, and all to no avail. God had to convict me of the correct path.

Our old affiliation made it's choice: they can be all things to all people. The true church can only be one thing: faithful and full of faith.

The decision to plant a church in Beaver Falls was the second tough decision to be made, we felt that this should be the role of all Christians – to spread the gospel to all places on earth (even in our own back yards). What was hard to face was that the existing dozens of churches in that area could not provide the right worship areas for His people, and this was proved by the great number of unchurched people. So far I believe God guided us in the proper direction.

Only time will tell if these various pruning's and plantings were the correct measures for us to take, but as in springtime when you see the verdant greening up of the fields and trees, I see joyful God loving people and, oh, so many children running around our church(es). I see parents of the children coming to our church because of their children. I just absolutely know God, for sure, did get it right and we just happened to listen for once.

I know we will continue to pray for our old affiliation, for our Lord to shape them and use them and mold them to fit His plan for salvation, and I absolutely know God loves all His children, no matter if they are as broken as me.

Chapter 6: Nicaragua Mission Trip

A number of my brothers at First Presbyterian Church contacted me and asked if I was interested in going on a mission trip to Nicaragua, several years ago. I had never really thought about it, but prayed about it and thought: well I think I do need to go and learn. I let them know that yes I did want to go. I was told then to write up an application and hand it in, so I did. We had numerous meetings before we departed, one with our wives. We also had a work session, doing some work around the church. I was pretty sure that Sue was not thrilled with me going – said I was too old. Well, I pretty much ignored that and went any way.

The worst thought on my mind was getting the shots we needed (I have had a phobia with hypodermics for many years), but got through it OK. We left on Saturday 2/28/2009, and I had to leave Sue, very sick with norovirus, throwing up over and over again. She got it from our grandson Ryan. The kids promised they would keep an eye on her, so we left.

When we left the church for the airport I will always remember one brother chasing the bus since he was not on it. We stopped several blocks away and let an out of breath brother get aboard.

When we got to Managua, Nicaragua, there were demonstrations going on in the streets, but we did not see any of these signs of unrest. It is a very poor city and lots of signs of sinfulness there.

At the airport, in Managua, I gave a $2 tip to the guys who loaded our suitcases on the bus. I got yelled at for this because I was told- doing this causes the flow of $'s to go out of whack (not sure what this meant), but I felt I had to be fair to them (after all they had just loaded 30 full suitcases).

Managua was one of the most depressing places I have seen. Filth, sin, and depression rampant, but ... Christians are in evidence. There is always hope, I think. We went by bus to the Nehemiah Center on the outskirts of Managua. There were very nice barrack style rooms there, owned by Food for the Hungry. They also have a school there for a lot of kids. A couple of people from their organization accompanied us during our stay in Nicaragua.

The next day was Sunday and it was a beautiful morning. I walked around the grounds there and saw a lot of chickens, birds, papaya, banana (plantains), and many new types of weeds, plus many guard dogs.

The first night sleeping was a little rough with no air conditioning and lots of sounds – birds, frogs, lizards, sirens, and roosters. But we made it through ok.

Rooster crowing began about 2 am and lasted through 8 am. I think they needed their clocks reset, or made into fried rooster.

We all (15 of us) took a bus to a church service in Managua (it was a charismatic service) and the Spirit was much in evidence, with a lot of action in their service (also drums, brass, etc.). We all held hands and prayed at one time, could not understand the words of the prayer, but I am absolutely sure the Spirit communicated what was said well enough. Puzzled by the American minister's service – seemed overly aggressive against the politics of Nicaragua.

We then had a brief tour of Managua before we ate lunch at a barbeque restaurant (not our kind of barbeque), but it was good. We saw an old government building (now a museum) and a statue to somebody, but I forget who. We saw lots of volcanoes in the area that you can see from high places. Lake Managua is huge (like a great lake almost), but it is totally dead from the debris that was pushed into it after the earthquake of 1979. We had coffee at lunch that was very good (Nicaragua is famous for it's coffee). We were presented with a film from Food for the Hungry about sponsoring a child. (this cost is $32 per month).

We then went on a ride to Chinandega, Nicaragua, about 2.5 hours away (north). We stopped about half way and looked at Lake Managua close up – absolutely no life. I got yelled at again when someone had the perception (wrongly) that at a rest stop I was buying stuff for myself. (I was only holding other people's stuff). I saw lots of mango and banana trees, horses pulling carts, rice paddies, even some fields guarded by huge hogs (no not dogs), and a lot of arid land (dry season). Note here that much of the land was poisoned during the 40's and 50's with chemicals used by the large farming companies raising cotton. The subsurface water is still not good to drink. It is horrible to see what uncaring people have done.

We got to the hotel about 7 pm – it was actually a large house with a center open section. Our rooms are all around the manor and we ate dinner there – mystery meat??

I got to call home from a corner internet shop owned by a Hungarian man. One of our men talked to him in Hungarian. They were probably the only 2 people in Nicaragua capable of having a conversation in Hungarian. They had 2 phones and 3 internet connections. I needed 6 calls to finally get through. I was doing something wrong. Sue was still pretty sick, but was slowly getting better.

For the next 4 days we spent the daylight hours working in El Limonal – past the local prison, past the town cemetery, past the city dump (that burns constantly and smokes out the people living in El Limonal) just about the worst conditions you can imagine. The people of El Limonal were given this land by the government when they were forced out of their homes by a volcano and mud slide. Our job(s) this year was to finish a termite-damaged building so a doctor could visit the village periodically. Also, to enclose the school (cement pads) yards with barbed wire fencing so the children could grow some vegetables. Also, a few people dug needy family toilet pits (latrines).

The school was filled with about 60 bright, glowing, happy children (3 to 11 years old). About half the kids ran up to us immediately full of love and a desire for communication. About half the kids stood back a little but not for long. By the end of the day there were no strangers there.

One man (actually very few men ever helped or talked with us), his name was Manual, came up later and began to help. Also another man, Carlos was the village leader who guided us in our work. Later in the day, Dave Diaz and I went with Manual and ministered to him on his need to improve his "house within" since he had a history of alcoholism. It was very heartwarming to see 16 grown men playing/loving all these children (the 16th was the bus driver). Everyone stayed hydrated pretty well. Several of the local teenagers jumped right in and began helping us dig latrines and hang fences.

A lot of the children in the area have worm infestations and have a difficult time making it through to adulthood, because their parents won't give the kids the medicine they need to kill the parasites. This hesitancy, plus the difficulty of getting the necessary medicine through the layers of government in the country, cost many an early death. It was really tough hearing this. Significant also, is the missing fathers (most are out gleaning from the city dump). I don't think many of the fathers actually have jobs – unemployment in Nicaragua is a majority. 2/3 of the people make less than $2 a day. There are about 5 women who do most of the work for the school. They were good Christian women, and they were the strength of the community. I called Sue daily and she was slowly improving.

It was absolutely amazing to see how happy the children were, even with the fact they had no toys. They had fun playing with each other and building relationships among themselves. We did have a bunch of 12 year olds following us around a lot. They were typical wise guys at the beginning, but after a while (and with Dave Diaz translating) they warmed up to us a lot and jumped in and helped us get work done.

We prayed a lot for the people, all the people, at El Limonal.

The last day we got 300 ice cream treats delivered by a man on a bicycle, and handed them out. I could not believe we ran out with 2 kids left out, but we gave them other treats. 300 kids in this little village!!!!

We had a Jesus movie projected on a sheet hung over the main street in the village one night. It was well attended (about 150 people). Dave Diaz stopped the projection half way and began to preach. 20+ people came forward and accepted Christ, one of them was the 12 year old gang leader, who helped us. Some people are gifted to help with their ability to preach, and obviously Dave is.

I was very thankful there were very few mosquitoes this time of the year.

I was amazed at one lady's house. She had a homemade light switch. Her brother had fabricated it out of a hypodermic needle. It occurred to me that it might have been used by a drug addict and she had turned this instrument of darkness into one of light.

We visited many houses in the village during several Prayer Walks. We would stop at a house (actually they were card board/sheet metal cubes) and stand and call out to the people inside. When they came out, we would ask if there was anything we could pray with them for? They always told us their needs and we would pray together. They were very moving experiences for all concerned. (I was later to try this in Ambridge and got the same moving results.) I would really like to see this done on a regular basis by all Christians in all areas.

I called Sue on March 5 and wished her a happy Anniversary. She was feeling better and ate some soup that day. Since I was kind of the medical watchman, I looked after possible injuries: total injury report for our effort was 15 boo boos, 2 muscle strains, 1 ringworm, and one man's broken heart (Brian) for having to leave behind all those beautiful children. We did give out some soccer balls, base balls and bats.

All in all, the trip was a very instructive one for me, especially spending time with brothers in Christ and doing needful help for the most needy, sharing devotionals between us on various subjects, and knowing that God works for good in all things, for those who love him. I learned the Holy Spirit is at work in us, connecting the men on this mission together in a unity, unfathomable the week before, plus having faith in each other and holding each other up as the need arose. I found prayer walks are a most wonderful way of uniting with even non-believers to help them know what we worship and why we worship cur most awesome God.

Chapter 7: Carpenter's CHORE

Several years before I reached retirement age, God once again called me to action – to begin an effort helping needy people in Beaver County with their houses – similar to what we had been doing for years in the Fix It Brigade, but a much larger effort. I thought at first there must be an organization already in place that would be accomplishing this cause. I checked with the Habitat for Humanity and found out they do this helping in some sections of the USA, but not Beaver County. I found no available help here at all. I did find a group working in a nearby county that put a group of churches together, and, one week a year, help any who request help. I spent a day there researching how they did this, and how effective it was. I talked to a lot of people in our church about possibilities and possible help.

I now needed a name for the organization; my first thought was Angels in Training. I felt called to begin training for my next job as a Guardian Angel – hah! My pastor quickly changed my mind and suggested another name from his last church. I could not find any information on this, so I let the whole thing stew in the back of mind since I thought the possibility of my retirement was pretty far down the roadway of time. Little did I accept, that all things are possible with God. A couple of years later, God had multiplied my 401K funds to the point that there was now a door I could go through, to where I should be. Another door opened at my work that allowed me to leave with grace. Another door opened that put a new name for the work – our new associate pastor, said "come up with a new name by tomorrow". And up popped Carpenter's CHORE (comfort and hope outreach and evangelism). Seemed pretty appropriate, and it began in April, 2009.

I worried a little bit about insurance and litigations but church insurance, and a liability release sheet for people to sign releasing us from responsibilities covered concerns. As it turned out the toughest part was locating people who needed help. We already had contacts with the Blind Association, the Office of Aging, Churches Serving Together (CAST), and several other volunteer organizations. Our effort started slowly with most clients from CAST. These people needing help were mostly widow ladies who were longing for someone to visit them, and the repairs were mostly painting, cleaning, and other small repair jobs. We did comfort the people we visited and always prayed with them.

One memorable project was for a lady in Ambridge with a son with problems (referred to us by the Pressley Ridge Institute), we fixed a number of items around her house (plaster, windows (5), door, paint, attic leak) then a number of us did a prayer walk around the neighborhood (like in El Limonal – see Nicaragua chapter) (there were about 6 of us including the lady we did the work for). We visited several houses: the first was a man who just moved in the area, we prayed with him and explained, we felt called to invite people back to church, if they had not been there for a while, and to relate that God missed them not being there. He admitted he had missed church for quite some time but would try to get back into going, he also stated he would like to go with us during our next prayer walk! The second person we visited was a lady who had just lost her son to drug overdose, she did not want us to pray for her, because she was still mad at God, but felt she would soon get over this. We invited her to our church's Celebrate Recovery ministry. The third person was a nice family that had 2 daughters, and they asked us to pray for their safety in this troubled area of Ambridge, and also for healing for her mother (kidney transplant). The fourth house was a family where the husband just got out of jail that day, and had to return in 2 more days for another crime. We prayed for and with all of them (even the husband who was there) they were very thankful, and I think more hopeful that before we talked.

This was our last prayer walk but not because of any lack of need. The reason I felt a need to stop these was all these people asked "where they could go to church, because they did not know of a good church near them" and we were at a loss to advise them except to invite them all the way to Beaver. Our church community around Beaver County (and

America) needs to change something to bring people back to church and worshipping our Lord.

Even the small tasks were rewarding for us. In the beginning there were about 3 of us and another 3 or 4 guys who would go with us, occasionally. Towards the end of the year, (we only work from April until November) we added Veteran's Affairs to our list of organizations. Our first request from Veteran's Affairs was for an 84 year old WW2 veteran who could not leave his home because he could not climb down stairs. His wife said she had called VA and they told her it would be 3 years until they could help. We visited and prayed with them and talked about the need with a couple of people at our church. It was absolutely amazing when one of the people said (he is a principle in an elementary school in Beaver) that he had some construction trailers that must be torn out, and one of them had a wheel chair ramp that must be ripped out. We measured it and it was exactly the right size. We disassembled it, and then reassembled it at the veteran's home, and the problem was solved. There is no doubt who was in control here, we did not have enough resources or knowhow to do this job, without help from our Lord (the wheel chair ramp was over 30 feet long).

The next request we got was from CAST in December (we had already shut down but....) it was to clean a wheel chair ramp in Aliquippa. The elderly lady here was worried about visiting nurses slipping on her ramp and getting hurt. We water blasted her ramp then installed slip resistant coverings. This lady, was a wonderful Christian lady who was a joy to meet, she was also blind and a multiple amputee. I found out she regularly sits on her porch and yells to passer-bys that Christ loves them (and other inspirational lectures). (Now also you have to remember that this is an extremely bad area of Aliquippa – looks like a bombed out area and many of the people going by had to be drug salespeople.)

This ended the first year; we had helped about 20 people. But I hope we had planted seeds in many other (families, neighbors, other contacts, and workers). We felt much relieved that all had gone well and not many injuries (little bangs, splinters, etc). But we had much more work to come in the future.

The second year we added the Salvation Army, Habitat for Humanity, Visiting Nurses, Mental Health, and even a few referred to us from people we had helped the first year. We had a retired professional plumber (Lou) join us. The work requests this year became more demanding and harder. We did cement repair (steps), drywall, plumbing, house jacks, some small electrical repairs, and lots of carpentry. We installed grab bars for handicapped people, we even installed plumbing to and from a bathroom for a lady that had not had a bathroom for 4 and ½ years (she did have a mud room toilet in the basement).

We did some garden work for a lady with a daughter that was a paraplegic. We prayed a lot and I know God smiled on us and the people we were helping. We helped a handicapped lady who was a minister and could not do much around her house and was facing a fine by the local officials because she had a pool that she could not take care of (we learned how to take apart a pool). We always give people a Bible when we do work there but this woman was a professional translator (in English, Greek, Hebrew and some other languages) and said, very tactfully, she had 13 active Bibles and did not need any more.

We helped a young handicapped man who's daughter was taken away from him because he did not have a livable home (it had no water- had frozen up the year before he bought it and he had no idea how to fix it) We put in new plumbing and fixed all the faucets in the house and both toilets. He and his new wife had no money and were eating only beans. His wife, while we worked there got a job at a fast food restaurant and was allowed to bring home leftover burgers. Their meals were definitely upgraded. Because of the burgers plus them finding a nearby deer road kill. (They did get their daughter back). We did a number of repairs on a widowed young lady's trailer. Her husband had been killed in the military. We worked with her brother and her dad and made the trailer a livable home for her and her kids. We always prayed with the people and gave Christ all the credit for the accomplishments that were done. We added another new organization: Adoption Center, a Christian adoption place, and installed upgrades to their bathroom and an office kitchen. We still had about the same people doing the work and thought this might be the next area we needed to work on.

The third year (2011) we had another mainstay helper come on board (Rick Galand) but lost one (Bob Singo) to knee/back/hip problems, old age maybe, but that's where most of us are. We also added a retired physician (Vic Siha). Bob still helps but only can do visiting. Tried selling our need to a local retired people's club but did not get hoped for help. We did start the year with help on our funding - we got a grant from the Beaver County Foundation (for $2500 per year for 2 years). This year was to be the year of the wheel chair ramp (we did 9 ramps and porches). The cost of some of these ramps was close to $1800. We get $2000 normally from FPC and also some donations but we spent close to $8500 that year. (FPC made up the extra from emergency funding). Guess our Lord God knew we needed funding this year more than more people!

Some of the jobs we did in 2011 were replacing a hot water tank, painting and scraping, replacing some inside and outside doors, anchoring a wall, and repairing the valve set on a tub/shower. A very heartening job was done cutting the grass and hedges for a lady in Aliquippa, now how can that be heartening? We were called to help her by her neighbor. Her neighbor said she had seldom seen the lady next door but knew she was an old Caucasian lady and her grass and hedges were grossly overgrown. She, being an African American, thought she might frighten the lady if she approached her to help her. So we called, and then visited the lady. I made sure to bring the neighbor with us to visit the elderly lady. She was thrilled that someone cared. Both ladies are Christians and were instant hits with each other. We cut the grass and hedges and cleaned up the outside of the house. Wonderful to see how God works, close up and personal.

I think I learned a lot from a failure we had. The Beaver County Office of Aging called us with a request to help an elderly lady in Monaca Heights. We called her and she said she couldn't let us in. Talked to her caseworker and she made arrangements for us to visit. We visited (and found the lady was a hoarder) looked at her needs and made plans. When we visited to do the work (fix a door and other minor stuff) she refused to let us in. (Think she was ashamed of her mess in her house). Thought how much like us was she, accepting God's help to come in to our heart and then locking him out, refusing to let him help us straighten out our heart's mess. But wait it get's better. A few months later the lady called and asked us to help her with her garage (the roof had collapsed). We visited and saw the repair was way beyond our capabilities. We did disconnect the electricity to the garage. She asked us if we knew anyone who could do the work. We gave her names of people we knew who could help but would need to be paid – they had families to support. She called them all and selected one to do the work. The guy did a fine job and soon her roof was back up and the job looked (I saw pictures) great. The problem was that the lady refused to pay the guy for his work because he did not listen to all her complaints (none really valid) and sometimes he smoked on the job. The last I heard of this case, it was headed for courts to settle. The lady I think refused to trust and held tightly to her possessions (all of them) and would not even pay for services rendered. Example of the idols people hold to.

We installed some surveillance equipment for a lady in Bridgewater who was having trouble with a neighbor, not sure if it helped, but she did feel safer, so who am I to wonder. We helped a former missionary and visited with him several times. His wife told us his story (blind, multiple heart surgeries, a number of strokes, amputations on his feet and worst of all a desertion by his first wife and best friend). His new wife said he was so depressed, she did not know what to do. I think our visits and prayers helped him greatly. My pastor Jeff suggests that when outgoing people become isolated they indeed can become depressed.

We did a lot of work for a grandmother who was trying to raise her granddaughter, she had no water in her house, well pump did not work, outside porch had collapsed, and other problems. We ran the water lines and fixed the porch, another church (Mt. Carmel) fixed her well pump. What was truly memorable about this project was her granddaughter telling us she would like us to come back to her house when they moved back in and put a pool in the back yard. She wanted us to her pool party.

The most memorable project though was when we put in a wheel chair ramp for a little boy with cerebral palsy in Rochester. He could not bring his wheel chair home from school, until he had a ramp. The ramp was to be 16 foot long with posts dug down 3 feet and 1 foot in diameter. We plotted the job and began digging the post holes (we got 5 dug and had nothing left in us to do the 6th – rocks and roots made the job insane). We (5 of us) were collapsed on the ground when we thought we had to pray. Within a couple of minutes of our prayer, we struck black loam throughout the hole we were trying to dig. We quickly finished the job in ease and wondered among ourselves why we had not prayed earlier (maybe 5 holes ago). When we finished the ramp the little boy asked us "couldn't any of us stay and play with him?" Boy that will stick with you for a long time. Saw the family recently near the mall and the lady said the ramp was a real blessing to them. They looked much less stressed than when we first met them.

Some other projects were putting in a wheel chair ramp for a family in a trailer in New Brighton, a man his wife and his daughter. The ramp that was there was flimsy, broken, and unsafe. We put in our style of ramp (design from the elementary school construction trailer) and the family said the ramp would be standing long after the trailer was gone. A note here that we asked to pray with them each day we worked there, we came by the next year to check our work and the husband asked us to come in and pray with he and his family. I think God wanted us to see our seed beginning to grow.

Another unforgettable project was for an elderly lady in Hookstown. She lived down a small overgrown country lane by herself in a trailer parked beside a collapsing old house. She was a retired school teacher who knew every family in the area. We did a number of repairs for her including replacing her easy chair (could not fix her old one – spring up through the seat. She knew every weed in her yard (that was very overgrown) and was one of the most fascinating people I ever met (not just because of her knowledge of weeds). She had a guard goose that watched everything we did, when I asked what the goose's name was, she looked at me like I was from Mars, and said "Goosie". We prayed with her and gave her a Bible that she said she would pass on to others. She keeps in contact with a lady in our church.

We built another wheel chair ramp for a double amputee man in Patterson Township. He had picked up one of those flesh eating bacteria that caused his doctor's to have to keep cutting. We put in a nice ramp that his son helped us to finish by putting a roll of shingle material on the surface (we adopted this method into our future ramps.) The man and his wife were a bastion of faith. We seem to learn a little from so many people but I know the real source of these bubbles of inspiration.

One of our last and largest project for 2011, (and I thought forever) was for an elderly lady from Aliquippa (Plan 11). Many had told her no ramp could be put on her house and she was very worried what she would do since her doctors had told her they were going to have to remove both her legs. We got an inspiration on how to do this job and put it in by early December. We prayed every day with her and met her sons (3 of them but all were disabled except one who declined to help us claiming to be a hazard to all around him.) During our work there the lady fell inside and her son who will forever be held accountable by her, because he threatened to put her in a home if she fell again. Everyone needs help but her son will someday realize he missed his chance one time anyway. The lady's ramp ended up over 51 feet long and we installed a cross underneath it that you can see very plainly from the church next door (The Church in the Round). Her ramp became the talk of the town especially with what God had done through a few old white guys.

We did about 40 projects during 2011 and saw our Lord in so many of our efforts. We received such joy in our labors it seemed unfair that we should not pay for the privilege of these labors.

One of our main stay guys, Ed Neiman, went off on another effort, this year, helping to build tables and bunk beds for needy organizations around the country and some overseas. Amazing what they get done and sent out from a church in New Brighton. However he still helps 1 day/week.

In 2011 and 2012 we added a new organization (Glade Run) this organization deals with troubled youths (and troubled families). All the projects we get from them seem to be very difficult to handle. They are the biggest challenges I have ever encountered. I see so much need in these families (and hopelessness). I pray for the organization to have guidance from our Lord to help these hurting people. Unfortunately we did not initially see much joy in the occasions of our work on these, but we did accomplish all that we were asked plus more. Just wish the troubled youths could have been around as we performed our work at these locations (most of the time kids are in school when we do work.)

Last year we had several calls for help from people that we had helped before. Not large repairs but just a plea for help. We always responded but did try to relate to them that we were an evangelistic organization and our mission was to provide help and comfort those we helped with prayer and gospel information and not to function as a full time repair service. I did not like telling people this because I feel it did not go over too well but our mission, is what we should continue. We plant the seeds, but we have to rely on God to grow them where he will.

We did about 30 projects in 2012 and did not spend nearly as much as 2011 (but only did a couple of ramps versus 9 in 2011.) One of our ramps, this year, was our largest at 70+feet, in Aliquippa again. We had a call from the daughter of a family with both parents handicapped (actually the father passed away during our second week of work there). The father was a retired pastor of The Church In the Round (near where we had built the ramp in 2011). We had some help from one their grandsons. The lad played football for a local college and his strength put us to shame and he joined in our joy of work. This ramp had to be kicked at 45 degree angles twice, an engineering feat I never thought we could do but it turned out very well. I even took a trip down it on a dolly (wheeled vehicle).

A project that sticks out in my mind this year was for an older couple, in Rochester. We did a number of repairs (fixed shower valves, new mail box, scrape and paint railings). We shared witnessing stories but the thing that really jumps out to me was the old guy told me when he was in the Marines during the Korean war, just before dawn the company chaplain called all the men together and told them that if any wanted to accept Christ as their Savior now was the time to do it because it could be their last chance, before that day's big battle, a lot of the men there including

Bob came forward. Isn't it amazing how sometimes horrific or suffering events have to be encountered to open us up to eternal salvation. I also learned that once you are a Marine you are always a Marine – this was the discussion between one our guys (Bob Hales also a former – still a - Marine) and the old guy we were helping. Another great discussion that took place was between the old lady there and a young lady who was helping us that day – they had a lot in common in losses that they had incurred. I really think they helped each other via talking. Just shows you Everybody Needs Help.

We did a number of repairs for immigrants (one family from Pakistan) and an elderly lady from Thailand. They were all Christians and were so very appreciative for the minor work we did. The Pakistani family had lost a number of their family to murder in Pakistan, they left everything to come to this country. God's church(es) have helped them greatly (Catholic, Lutheran, Methodist, and Presbyterian), it is so wonderful seeing churches working together, after all we all work for the same Boss.

We did a rebuild and repair a porch and wheel chair ramp in Beaver Falls for a handicapped elderly lady. Her old construction was in pretty bad condition. We prayed and witnessed to the lady. We had a discussion about watching little kids (had told her of a picnic the day before when a lot of little kids were climbing trees and all the husbands/fathers were sent to collect them.) The woman (being African American) said she and all her family have never had that chance since all the husbands in the family, left their families, and only the women are left to these duties. Again too often there is a missing person in families – both men and women have their responsibilities and if either is missing, something is missing in child rearing (either respect or love, and both are absolutely necessary). Our Lord teaches us so much but it sure is hard, sometimes, to listen.

Our most physically painful project this year was a referral from the Office of Aging for an elderly lady, in Aliquippa. The work was fairly simple – trimming hedges, fixing hand railings, cutting some small trees out of her hedges. The pain was encountered in the hedges (about a million yellow jackets inhabited these hedges and it was a very hot day (makes them even angrier). I stirred them up and ran but got hit a couple of time and lead the swarm to the other guys – they got stung also (think they really liked Vic Siha (or Egyptian food - Vic is of Egyptian descent). I emptied 2 cans of wasp spray on them but did not bother them too much. Returned the next week with 3 large cans and finally annihilated them. Not sure why God put yellow jacket here but there must be a reason, probably something to do with suffering making people better.

We had a referral from Habitat for a handicapped older lady living in a trailer in Chippewa. She had purchased the trailer for a dollar – it was a shell. Her son from Ohio had been helping her as much as he could but she had no hot water (for two years now). We put a hot water heater and piping into her home and hooked it up to kitchen and bath faucets. She was ecstatic. She seemed to always have neighbors over to her house and many of them were as hurting as she is. One young man (who was missing a leg) they called Ihop. All wonderful people, who, we prayed with and swapped inspirational stories. A couple of days after we finished work there, the lady called and told us she had had a dinner (spaghetti) for her neighbors to celebrate her hot water. She said she was showing everyone what a great job these old guys (with God's grace) had done and that they were only amateurs. Ihop said well think about it – the Titanic was built by professionals and the Ark was built by amateurs.......

We had another referral from Habitat that comes to mind, a lady in Hopewell. She was a recently widowed elderly lady with many physical problems. We mowed her grass, replaced a bi-fold door, fixed a couple of other things around her yard and house, and got rid of poison ivy around her yard. She shared with us her financial problems and we gave her advice and some literature from the BC Office of Aging. She had a Lowry Organ in her basement that she said she wanted to sell but no one wanted to buy it, I asked her what she wanted for it - $100. I said I would buy it if she didn't have anyone else that wanted it. Ended up with it and my wife said "do not bring it home", so we donated it to the Aliquippa Salvation Army. They use it in their youth music outreach program, and frequently in the church services. Isn't it great how God works in his interweaving???

We had two more main stay workers join us this year in Bob Hales and Dave Blair. So many times now, we go out with 4 people, it sure makes the work easier and even more fun. God has blessed us for 4 years now and so many seeds planted. Put in another application for 2 more years of grants, also Habitat wants to talk to us this year about partnering with us. Let me put in a little blurb on our guys: they are in no certain order but mostly all retired, a chemical engineer, a chemical technician/foreman, an aircraft mechanic, a plumber, an electrical engineer/manager, a doctor, a glass factory worker, a financial advisor, a logistics expert, a college student, a fireman, a mall/property investor, a zinc salesperson, and many other varied backgrounds. Wow!! And we all get along, mostly, but only under our Lord's guidance.

I have to add a little story here about the trailer park where we installed a hot water tank. Recently, we were back to this park and visited a nice older widow lady who we will be helping when the weather improves. She told us, about 6 years before the park had a power outage that lasted far too long (about a week). Nobody in the park really knew one another but this event provided the impetus for them all to meet and share meals with (a lot of thawing foods to get rid of). After all the sharing of food, time, companionship; they all now are like one big family and help each other frequently (as much as they can since they are all pretty handicapped in some ways) but they do help one another. See we all need help, and can most assuredly, be a help to others.

God's Love is Free. No Strings Attached.
What we Offer is Free. No Strings Attached.

The Carpenter's
CHORE Program

(Comfort & Hope Out Reach Evangelism)

CHORE is a Christian out reach ministry to surrounding Beaver County communities. We receive referrals for help through Churches are Serving Together (CAST), the Office on Aging, the Blind Association, and other helping organizations. Our purpose is to help people who are unable to do necessary small projects due to physical or financial limitations. If you need help, or want to volunteer and serve with one of our teams, call 724-774-6398, extension 10, and ask for CHORE to contact you.

God so loved the world that he gave his one and only son, that whoever believes in him will not perish, but have eternal life.
John 3:16

To Receive This Gift:
Lord Jesus, please come into my life and be my savior and Lord. Forgive my sins and give me the gift of eternal life that you promise. In Jesus' name.

Lend A Hand:
Paint & patching (small jobs), yard work, small repairs, cleaning & hauling, fixing porches, plus other tasks (sorry but we don't do major construction, major plumbing, roofing, electrical work)

CHAPTER 8: HELPING/ACTIONS

As we have discussed many times, there are a huge number of ways we can help others. I will try to list a few. You can help most people just by talking with them and even mainly listening to them (I think most people need a hearer there so they can really hear themselves), another way is by praying with them – especially if you ask them first what you can pray with and for them for. There are, oh, so many volunteer organizations just begging for volunteers, just look and jump in. Churches have a huge number of committees and efforts to help people in their congregations and outreach efforts. If you look around you can see many (if not most) people have needs they cannot attain (food, housing, transportation, money, etc.) can you help? While traveling around our smaller and smaller world keep your eyes open for someone you can help or thank someone who helps you – that can be a great help to both of you.

As we found out in Carpenter's CHORE the toughest thing to find when you start out is finding someone to help. If you are ready to help someone, I guess you have found a need in yourself to help, so you need help. Complicated isn't it? Or maybe not.

There are missions galore in our churches, communities, neighborhoods, libraries, magazines, just everywhere. Get involved. There are even animal sanctuaries out there that need help, after all God put us on earth to be managers of the animals and the environment we live with and in. Take your responsibilities seriously and get to work (help them and by doing so you will help yourself.) Hospitals and nursing homes many times need volunteers, how about the Salvation Army or Red Cross, your local library? We just visited a big cat sanctuary near Amelia Island, they used all volunteers. The Bible tells us in Colossians 3:17 whatever you do in word or deed, do all in the name of the Lord Jesus, giving thanks to God the Father through Him.

I am very pleased to see my kids getting involved and volunteering. I have no doubt some day to see my grandkids too. Thank you my Lord for so many blessings and work for us to do.

In my beginning, as a Christian, came faith and recognition that there was a Supreme Being. This was followed by a hunger to learn more about our God. This led to finding that our God actually took action and came to lead us in human form – Christ. As I learned more about the Word of our God, I found that, with knowledge, comes a need (for us all) to take action. My training over the years has been a great help to understand this need (and the resultant actions).

Some verses from the Bible that help to understand the actions and directions for us (both individually and in church groups) are:

Matthew 5:14-16 You are the light of the world. A city on a hill cannot be hidden. Neither do people light a lamp and put it under a bowl. Instead they put it on it's stand, and it gives light to everyone in the house. In the same way, let your light shine before men, that they may see your good deeds and praise your Father in heaven.

1 Thessalonians1:6-12 As apostles of Christ we could have been a burden to you, but we were gentle among you, like a mother caring for her little children. We loved you so much that we were delighted to share with you not only the gospel of God but our lives as well, because you had become so dear to us. Surely you remember brothers, our toil and hardship; we worked night and day in order not to be a burden to anyone while we preached the gospel of God to you.

What these verses say, is to give light and effect to our efforts we must act and demonstrate, to our fellow human beings, how God has affected our lives through his gospel. Faith and knowledge are only the first steps (the eternal gift), that needs to lead to a growing realization of the next step - action (or service). Just as Jesus gave us his body and his blood, as reflected in communion, we are called to BE and DO as Christ has shown us. In Matthew 16:24 Christ tells us to follow Him. This definitely requires us to take action!

Our growth, as Christians, begins with the story of the gospel and the sure knowledge of the Word. With the growing fruits of Christianity comes a love of our fellow mankind and a need to be fruitful by spreading the Word of God. This immersion and conversation with our fellows will lead inevitably to conflict. Many of the lessons, of the past years, give me assistance in understanding how to deal with some of these conflicts, in order to get the Word of God to those who may not know it. This action and communication is called our service. The content of this service varies greatly with our various gifts, and tasks of service and stewardship, as we walk our walk to the end of our lives.

Many verses of the Bible, from beginning to end, deal with being fruitful. A few are:

Genesis 1:28 (Adam) Be fruitful and increase in number;
fill the earth and subdue it.

Genesis 9:7 As for you (Noah) be fruitful and increase in number;
multiply on the earth and increase on it.

Colossians 1:10 (to brothers) that you may walk worthy of the Lord,
fully pleasing Him, being fruitful in every good work and increasing
in the knowledge of God.

Matthew 7:16 You will know them by their fruits.

2 Corinthians 9:10 (serving with one's gifts) Now may He who supplies seed
to the sower, and bread for food; supply and multiply the seed you have sown
and increase the fruits of your righteousness.

James 3:17-18 (brethren) But the wisdom that is from above is first pure,
then peaceable, gentle, willing to yield, full of mercy and good fruits, without
partiality and without hypocrisy. Now the fruit of righteousness is sown in
peace by those who make peace.

John 15:2 (Christ's word) Every branch in Me that does not bear fruit
He takes away and every branch that bears fruit He prunes; that it may
bear more fruit.

John 15:8 (Christ's word) By this My Father is glorified, that you bear much
fruit; so you will be My disciples.

John 15:16 (Christ's word) You did not choose Me; but I chose you and appointed you that you should go and bear fruit; and that your fruit should remain; that whatever you ask the Father in My name He may give you. These things I command you, that you love one another.

Romans 7:4 (brethren) Therefore, my brethren, you also have become dead to the law through the body of Christ, that you may be married to another – to Him who was raised from the dead, that we should bear fruit to God.

Galatians 5:22 But the fruit of the Spirit is love, joy, peace, longsuffering, kindness, goodness, faithfulness, gentleness, and self-control.

Reading all the above verses shows an overriding theme that is: a call to action for us to serve our Lord by proclaiming His name and Word in some kind of help effort or service. This IS our calling: to join with others along with our families, in love, to share and show God's love and story of redemption. This is truly being fruitful in the manner our Lord meant us to be; not in a worldly manner but spiritually.

Being called to take action for Christ initiates our realization that God wants us to pursue some function – this is the beginning of our service. There then needs to follow a self-examination that includes a series of steps: questioning/exploration, analysis (inductive/deductive), prayer, studying scripture for help, meditation; all to identify the direction of our actions (where we can help). These directions should depend in a great deal on the gifts that God has given us, the doors that are opened to us, and the guidance that is revealed to us in the preceding steps.

When we are called to serve (and we all are), God has given us gifts for us to use in His service. It may take a good deal of effort for us to know and grasp what our gifts are. God may even change or add to our gifts as time goes on. Some of the gifts mentioned in Romans 12 are: prophesy, serving, teaching, encouraging, contributing, leading, showing mercy. Other gifts we have discussed are: wisdom, knowledge, faith, healing, miraculous powers, speaking, interpreting. These listings are by no means all of the gifts God can give us. Most importantly, the gifts that we are given must be used and developed with humility and wisdom, through trial and error with validation by your fellow Christians. We should be continuously inventorying our gifts and affirming them. Ready at all times to adapt them to changing challenges that we will encounter. Using these gifts in service to God, for others, will ultimately require us to be courageous in that service. Christ tells us in

Matthew 6:24 "If anyone would come after me, he must deny himself and take up his cross and follow me." Our cross is our gifts used in His service, action taken.

A great example of service that we should all consider is leading a small group Bible Study. Studying and understanding God's Word, and helping others to do the same, is a real goal of ministry service. Some of the facilitating steps to growing these studies would be to: (1) teach the group disciplines of love – for example by sharing life stories, listening and praying with each other, and /or responding to crises in each other's lives; (2) teach the group disciplines of community – for example by self discipline, care giving, humility, and/or being truthful; and (3) being good stewards of resources – for example by keeping to schedules.

Following God's guidance, as a church body, in taking action and using our gifts has, unfortunately, been a lack of much of modern society. The failure of the church in this has resulted in many of today's problems: moral decline, psychological problems, our focus on possessions, sexual immoralities, a lack of trust in anything, and on and on. Many churches along with other organizations made up of broken people (all of us) result in: power conflicts, building organizations bound up by rules and laws, despot-run organizations run by one or only a few individuals, or an organization continually changing style through a never ending series of "programs" like a revolving door.

Our only answer to dealing with the impending moral disaster is by turning back to Christ for leadership. He is our only answer. Recognition of this answer is the first step. Taking actions in God's service are the next steps for us all. God will supply the rest.

Before discussing our Christian beliefs with someone, that other person should have a grasp of who we are as Christians (followers of Christ). A prolegomena (note: I have been waiting for 2 years to use this word, but have to use it 2 more times before it is mine.) statement or discussion would seem to be absolutely necessary to allow for communications to take place, in a time frame that would at all be possible to sustain.

My prolegomena (this is a big word that is a list, outline of basic attributes or suppositions of any thinking system including theology; and is to help us understand and emphasizes coherence) statement: God created the universe and all that is in it, including time and space. Christ is one with God the Father. He came to earth to mend the relationship between God and mankind. He voluntarily went to the cross with all of our sins, was resurrected on the third day and represents us to God the Father when judgment day comes.

In the beginning all God made was good, even very good. God as a creator is perfect in every way; His creation described in the Bible is like an infinite tapestry being woven in time and space with all creation put into perfect order. But man, being young and untried, failed and fell from his relationship with God, we were broken. We, humans, being managers of the earth, federal headship principles dictated that the entire kingdom was broken. God being the perfect Father (we were made in the image of God and are like his children) had the perfect method of correcting his children; this method would require a lot of time, effort, and pain to bring to close the brokenness. (This plan was indeed part of His tapestry). But remember, our Father absolutely does not want to throw out any of us (the wheat) with the chaff (the people who seek only the darkness). So He goes to great lengths to do the loving act and help for us.

Many times people try to bring up Satan or fallen angels and the power they have had to bring about man's fall, and actions God has taken to "defeat" Satan. I think, God is so far above angels (including Satan), because they also are creations of God. God's plan and creation of the universe, undoubtedly, has a place and purpose for them. I am sure they are following God's plan and purpose to a "T " even if they might think otherwise. What their story is we don't need to know, everything we need to know about God's story is in the Bible.

Being a parent gives one a perspective of the requirements necessary to shepherd your children from infancy to adulthood. The discipline (both positive and negative discipline) are not easy to administer, meter, or judge effectiveness and direction. The old saw that "this is going to hurt me more than it hurts you" is certainly true, but the love one feels when you see your child walking the path he should, also certainly shows the value of the effort one puts into their upbringing. God probably felt this when Jesus was baptized by John the Baptist, when he said "this is my Son in whom I am well pleased."

The mending of the relationship between God the Father and mankind is called atonement (in English – the word was translated from Latin by William Tyndale in 1534 – he had to fabricate a word since the concept did not exist in English. The word was actually formed from "at one ment".) This atonement is completely God driven and exists only by His grace. I think there were a number of interwoven reasons and results in God's plan of grace, as God so beautifully interweaves all of creation. I believe phase one was to mend the relationship on God's side.

God designed this from the beginning of our brokenness and during many events in Biblical times. For instance, from the very beginning sacrificial substitution was shown in Genesis when many animals had to be sacrificed to provide Adam and Eve with clothing. Another example was when the entire first born of Egypt had to be sacrificed to free the Jews from enslavement. Yet another example that was provided, with a twist, was Abraham and Isaac – instead of Isaac being sacrificed to God, God provided a substitute (a spotless ram) to be sacrificed. This history of substitutional sacrifice provided a pathway to be followed in scripture for God the Father to send God the Son to substitute for our punishment (necessary sacrifice.) This substitutional sacrificing of his only Son also shows the tremendous love God has for us.

Phase 2 of God's plan can be called The Moral Influence Theory (by many theologians). The result of Christ's going to the cross exhibits to all mankind, God's overwhelming love of man. This example of love, along with the spiritual influence from the Holy Spirit - softens hard hearts of many of humankind. God is well aware of who the elected people are, or will be, and who will be softened and brought into the path to salvation in Christ. The Bible, when read with the realization of it's trustworthiness, shows such an infinite hand guiding the unfolding story up to, during, and after Christ's crucifixion. The Bible is the book of Christ and the basis of all our beliefs and our church.

Many churches today have lost their way because they have slowly moved towards worldly concerns, poor leadership (egos), faith in things besides scripture (science), or emotional tensions. In my lifetime Christian faith has decayed unbelievably to a point that Christians are being persecuted in many areas around the world (even in areas of America).

I am absolutely sure that the above statement will stir controversy with whoever the discussion is being held with, but controversy shows care and interest in my mind. With an open mind, communications can take place. The facts of scripture are so trustworthy that an open mind will, in the end, realize the truth that is in the gospel. I have no doubt God the Holy Spirit, can and will do the rest if He feels it is righteous to do that.

One of the most tried and true mission tools for Christianity is through Christian men and women exhibiting the faith and love that our Lord has poured into and onto us. We have always overflowed this caring onto all those around us. This is only an example of being "in Christ", putting his attributes onto our selves, walking his path.

This (the above) is the biggest help we can give to others, act and follow our Lord and Savior.

Thought in closing: let us labor for our Lord and Savior and let Him produce more laborers to harvest all, for with the right plantings, fertilizers, and watering, and with God's help – all (or at least more) men may be saved and come to the knowledge of the truth. AMEN.

Chapter 9: Our Future and Grandkids

Our future, on this world, is represented by those we leave behind. Our children, grandchildren, those we have impacted or helped, and those we have helped to learn, those we have shared with, and so many contact points between us and the rest of the world. The movie, "Wonderful Life", comes to mind. Jimmie Stewart had no idea of how much he influenced his world until he was removed from it. The same is surely true of all of us. This influence can be either positive or negative, it is our choice. Christ is the ultimate example of what one man can accomplish. Our eternity is deeply influenced by his short time on this earth.

What is truly amazing when you look at our lives is how we are affected by our children and our grandchildren and all those people we interact with. That is to say as much as we try to influence others, we are influenced by them. Once again, we reach a point where it becomes so complicated we are at a loss to understand. These relationships between all humans become another awesome example of the interweaving that the Lord our God has created. He has chosen us for our tasks and gifted us with our abilities and sent us on our missions. We perform as we choose and are rewarded far beyond what we deserve. Now keep in mind that the stress level we possess abates greatly when and if, we remember and trust in God to handle most of the difficulties.

I will use my children and grandchildren for an example of the grace of our Lord. I have 2 children, Angela and Paul, 3 grandchildren, Matthew, Cannon, and Ryan. I did not plan or deserve any of the above but without any of them, my life would be so greatly diminished that unbearable pain would be borne. My Lord chose me before I was born and had to go to great strides to awaken this knowledge in me, just in time to see what my eldest grandson and daughter were about to go through (over 3 years of fighting Leukemia). I witnessed so many miracles during this period I cannot even begin to list them. Also I witnessed the depth of heroism that a young child and a family can come up with, it numbs the senses. I love my daughter but never thought she could possibly come up with the love, to walk through the 3 years of struggle that she so wonderfully did. If you have any doubt as to the existence of our Lord you have only to witness how this young family lived through this period and your doubt will disappear. On Chemo side-effects there occurred the worst (blood clots, kidney stones, along with the "expected" ones of nausea, hair loss, aches, pains, drop foot.) I think the most amazing sight though, was the birth and growth of faith in the entire family. You really don't normally see faith exhibited in a 4 year old but I saw it in spades. Even the occurrence of, witnessing to others, in and out of the hospital. My grandson to this day is different than most kids his age but to his credit. Most kids of 8 have not yet fully accepted Christ as their Lord but Matthew has. Now keep in mind that this world will not love Christian faith, or Christians, or Christian behavior, thus Matthew many times has difficulty. I only pray that this difficulty will diminish in time as others around him grow in their faith.

My second grandson was born after many years of extraordinary efforts by my son and daughter in law. They had to use the most scientifically advanced efforts, to which God has gifted the world, to allow Cannon to be conceived, grown, and be birthed. What a truly loving little guy he is. His joy in living is a wonder to all around him. His growth in knowledge and skill and gifts is outstanding. He is another loving little fellow who just truly loves all those around him. I once again saw our Lord involved when Cannon developed an abscess behind his eye. I saw how God works through people (his parents, the Doctors at Children's hospital, and many others) the problem was promptly recognized, treated, and he recovered very well. Not sure if everyone recognized the severity of the problem and what could have happened without all the steps taking place quickly. Again I give our Lord thanks for the entire correction.

My third grandson Ryan, Matthew's brother, took an actual village to get through his first 3 years (during Matthew's treatments). He is a vivacious, outgoing, loving person to everyone he meets. He knows no strangers. He is so confident, and I am at loss to understand how this could have happened, but I know somehow God was involved, as always. I do also know that he is an absolute joy for his parents and a great comfort at many times. I also know there was great fear as he approached his fourth birthday (leukemia has a higher incidence in siblings, and many times occurs around 4 years old, and I know Angela knew this). But that birthday passed as did the next one and now hopefully the next one. I again give our Lord thanks for this passing, yet another example of help we received.

These 3 young people are prime examples of what is right in our futures. There is truly hope and God has provided them to us. They are truly shining stars in my life. That is not to say they are angels for certainly they are not. They are, however, people who will walk a long walk to be with our Lord. I absolutely know, God will guide them in this walk. Cause after all, everybody needs help!

I think we should all look around at those young and old, near and far, no matter how pretty or not; and think to ourselves how can we help them? What would our Lord have you do to help them? How can we just stand by and ignore a need? How can we witness an 8 year old, reach out and help, and allow ourselves, as adults, to just stand and look away from need? Remember. Love. Help.

I have been blessed with the chance to help out in the CBS (Community Bible Study) children's bible study a few times. The unbelievable witnessing of how much those kids grasp – far beyond most of us – is most gratifying. You can really see God working through these kids. With our Lord in control, do not worry, just follow where he leads.

In CLI studies, I learned from one of our guest pastor/teachers that some where around 80% of people who come to Christ, do so before they are 18 years old and around 90% before they are 21 years old. So please take heed and get your children involved in a Christian education before they drift into a lost area and have to be rescued by more onerous measures. But I really feel the best we can do is to show them in our actions, of us following Christ. Kids really do learn more from our actions than from our words. One only has to review the testimonies I have included to verify this fact.

Chapter 10: Government Failures

Up to now, I occasionally mentioned how our various governments have tried to help people in need and how some programs have worked out for us. But now let's go more intentionally into this review.

Being of a senior age, I now have experience with Social Security. I never, in the past, thought this was a necessary government activity. Who is the government to force us to save money for our retirement? Surely most, if not all, people save for this time in their lives. NOT! I think actually a majority of people never get to the point of saving money for their old age. I know not their total living expense. I see so many of our elderly people really struggling. I have actually met many who live on only a few hundred dollars per month and all that is from Social Security. So maybe the idea of government taking this responsibility on themselves is not all bad. The down side, it seems to me, is that, as in most other programs, the government doesn't know when to stop. They just take a good thing and keep trying to politicize it until it becomes a failure. First they added Medicare to it, then they added people who are injured or ill, then many, many others. They try to patch up the system, as they cause it to near failure, but never seem to get it at a balance point.

How like us is our government? We are blessed with something and then want more. We actually end up just expecting the blessings and get upset when we don't receive them. Throughout the Old Testament you can see this fact reflected in the history of the Jewish people. They were blessed by God and then became rich and powerful, drifted away and forgot who was blessing them, became spoiled and resentful when the blessings stopped, then collapsed in weakness and moral decay. It sure seems to be happening to our country today.

I have thought, for a long time, that America is truly blessed and God has continuously guided us and our leaders. Our forefathers were allowed to cross the ocean (similar to the Jews crossing the Red Sea and the river Jordan, and maybe the Rio Grande today) to a promised land. They come to start a new life. God uses his people to spread his word. (missionaries, military, business). Our fathers were sent to protect freedom and God's people, in Europe, Asia, and Africa, all around the world. We have at times not been victorious in our military or business or mission work, immediately, but have always seemed to plant seeds that God has grown to achieve exactly what he wants in places that man could not possibly envision. Perhaps man's history is another wonderful interweaving of God's hand?

How about all the areas the government spends on: energy, education, housing, commerce, drug enforcement, alcohol, tobacco, and firearms, finance, and an absolute host of other efforts. How about they just lump them together under Miscellaneous?? I haven't really seen a lot of accomplishments here but again I look at them from a distance, not sure how many of these are a Yes, but...

I have always thought the role of government is to protect us – from the packs of wolves that is international governments. This is, or I think, should be, the role of our federal government. The role of state and local government I have always thought is to also protect us from the individual wolves out there preying on people.

I have since learned through my experience in business that our environment can be in danger from a different set of wolves (businesses). I was lucky enough to work for very progressive companies, mostly, and they fully fulfilled all legal obligations to be good environmental citizens and even a little extra. But I have seen other businesses that were not quite so responsible. They did not even follow existing laws, simply ignoring them. Some have actually had individuals, in their business that broke the law and dumped hazardous chemicals into the environment. So maybe we do need a federal and/or state government that controls this type of "pack of wolves."

Another "pack of wolves" is many of the big businesses that exist in most business areas. They indeed are predatory in their behavior. Perhaps we do need some kind of protection from their behavior. (This could cover communications, farming, retail, banking, stock markets, and a host of other human interrelations. Maybe we do need more government than I first thought. There are indeed many types of predators at our doors and we really do need help with many of them.

But many of the jobs that government has taken on have resulted in damaging many people in our country and around the world. They have replaced churches and neighborhoods in being the first source of help. This has resulted in collapses of help techniques that survived for millennia. People pay taxes to the government and think "they", the government, now take on the burden of helping people, and so stop their actions. People just don't realize helping others is one method that God uses to help us grow. If we stop action in our growth we are as a result stunted and decay. If we act as our Lord would have us, our progression to sanctity continues and we are indeed blessed. Our action of help can be designed, differently, to help each individual, and then less waste of help results. Individuals needing help, know the people helping them; and do not feel they have to fabricate stories to gain help, and show appreciation to the helpers and to our Lord. All are blessed. In contrast, if the government hands out help, the people needing help are many times demeaned, forced to make up hard luck stories, families divorce or some other method of separation, governments in power are kept in power out of fear of loss of help and become rubber stamps of poor performance (and no fresh, inspired efforts are produced.)

Even in international helpings we have failed. We have dumped help in dollars, food, clothing, weapons, and other "stuff" on people who only want a hand up to being self-sufficient. A few people in those lands become hugely rich but most stay poor or become poorer (for example how about farmers in countries where we dump free food, or clothing makers where we dump clothes??) In most of the international dealing we take on, we put out an attitude of superiority in all that we do. (We know how you should act and we only reward you if you "sit up" and do what we want. Or we will pay you to be our friend.) Wow, we may have our hearts in the right place but have probably disconnected our brains. I don't think this is the kind of help our Lord had in mind when he blessed us with so much. God not only gave us blessings in stuff but he has given us blessings in brains, hearts, and just common sense, let's use them all and get input from all sections of our society.

I think it was Winston Churchill who said "Show me a young conservative and he has no heart. Show me an old liberal and he has no brain." I always thought that statement was spot on, now as I'm really old

I think that might not be entirely true. I have become a "Yes, but...." and maybe a bit of a no brain person but then maybe I always was.

Thoughts of: the damage done to huge areas by radioactive poisoning (in Russia, Japan, and America), the poisoning of the land and water in Nicaragua, the reports of the damage to the Aral Sea area in Russia, the damage in Kazakhstan from power plants dumping ash into their lakes and miners dumping tailings everywhere, my seeing Alaska between the 1960's and 2001 – the unbelievable disappearance of glaciers – global warming is absolutely true (maybe not the cause but it is warming), the increase in desert areas everywhere (overgrazing, warming, diverting water, other causes), the huge increase in autism caused by who knows what, the introduction of genetically modified foodstuff into our foods, the reports of chem-trails in the sky from plane exhausts, the experiences I have seen with anti-depressants, tranquilizers, and pain killers, and the list goes on and on. All this can overwhelm a person.

My real fear is the scope of control that governments have obtained. I always think of the closing of the Lord's Prayer (For You (Lord)are the kingdom, the power, and the glory), my thoughts are that man or men or governments have not and should not be allowed to possess too much kingdom, powers, or glories – they cannot control their ego's enough to possess them. They seem to always be corrupted by them.

As less people in the world acquire more and more sway over all the above things, the danger of abuse is magnified – just imagine the dangers possible in: nuclear weapons, geo engineering (weather control or massive changes on or in the earth), genetic manipulation of plants or animals or even people, bio engineering of bacteria or viruses, human psycho-therapeutic treatments and controls. The list is beyond my imagination so please use yours if you dare.

But what do you do? We need a government don't we? The only hope I see is to hand over control of our kingdom, our power, and our glory to our Lord. And the only way I can think to do this is by making sure that all information is open, yes all; to all voting peoples, so that they can make informed decisions and their faith in our Lord can guide enough people to make decisions that are the right ones in God's guidance. I can only pray that God's Will can sway enough to provide a majority decision in the vital matters that face the world today. God is my hope. Our way is clear – follow Christ. And above all pray!

You see everybody needs help – even the world and the most powerful governments. And by helping - you help yourself.

CHAPTER 11: NOT ALL HELP HELPS

Our Domestic Mission Team uses and studies a book written by good Christian men –Steve Corbett and Brian Fikkert - the name of the book is "**When Helping Hurts**". The authors have spent their lives helping the poor in various efforts (both working and in teaching efforts). Their book brings up a number of times and conditions when the efforts from a mission trying to help people in some place in the world hurt the people they were trying to help. Their suggestion is to do homework before giving help, such as, getting to know the people you are trying to help, be aware of their psychological, spiritually, social, and other positions, and especially the relationships that these people have with God, themselves, others, and their environment. Knowledge of these relationships can give us guidance of what kind of help we can (and should) offer; and they absolutely must be involved in most of the decision-making.

Many times people of the modern world think they inherently know best what to do in all circumstances. This is actually a rather arrogant stance and is demeaning to the people in the society we would like to help. Sometimes the help we offer actually hurts the way they live. They (the authors) give us a lot to think about and actually give us many tools to use when we begin an effort. I have tried since reading their book to apply it to our efforts in Carpenter's CHORE but I am still not sure all our efforts are always a positive help.

One of the first steps before truly helping someone - is to get to know them, to build a relationship. And then get to know what help they

need. This book ("**When Helping Hurts**") suggests 3 types of help and depending on which type, the person responsible and the work varies. There is help of an emergency type (relief), help of a rehabilitation type, and there is help of a developmental type. Relief help is an urgent and a temporary fix aimed at immediately reducing suffering from a crisis. Rehabilitation help begins as soon as the bleeding stops and seeks to restore situations to a pre-crisis state. Developmental help is an ongoing work to improve people life situations.

Remember development help is not done to people or for people, but with people. This type help promotes empowering the people.

The problem with most American churches is they apply relief in situations where developmental or rehabilitation help should be applied.

The motive of developmental help is for the local people to take charge of their needs and their communities' needs. This type help should only be done if they absolutely need your help, otherwise you could be doing harm.

We should always keep in mind to avoid paternalism, which is, doing things for people that they can do for themselves.

The goal we should keep in mind is to pursue the process of walking with people who are materially poor, so that they become better stewards of their own lives and property.

Most organization, however, focus on relief because: they have a material definition of poverty, it is easier than development, it is easier to raise the money for the project, or any of a large list of drivers to get the job done. Remember the saw that it is easier to give a man a fish than to teach him to fish, but with the first you have to keep feeding him and with the later he can feed himself forever.

The large point here is that as you build the relationship by working with the poor, you have a much greater chance of growing people into a long-term discipleship to Christ.

What is truly impressive in this book ("When Helping Hurts") is the sincerity that is easily seen in their writing. They have since written a second edition and added many more guidance's and tools that can be used by people trying to help others that may be in need of help. The authors actually have looked at feedback from others about their book and addressed questions that they received.

They also consistently give our Lord credit for their guidance's. One of their tools describe before help is offered and developed, that the helper needs to repent and humble himself. After all, how can we help

others if we only seek to help ourselves? And how can we build up others if we only seek to enlarge our own egos?

I would very much advise anyone or group hoping to help someone or some group, to study this book and make it your own before beginning. And if you already have studied the first edition, follow this up with the second edition.

Chapter 12: Personal Lifetime Relationships

In Genesis 2:24 God gave us a helper (a wife or, presumably, a husband). God used parts (a rib) to form the other (I presume to the modern world this would mean each – wife or husband – is made of parts from the other.)

In 1 Corinthians Paul tells us it is better if we do not need a helper but if we can't get by without one then be married and thus have a helper (I assume this to mean sexually control yourself and if unable then get married and not try to get "help" from people we are not married to).

In Ephesians 5:25 Paul again tells us that if we are married then husbands have the responsibility to love their wives as Christ loved the church (even to the point of giving his life). Wives have the responsibility to respect their husbands as the church respects Christ (and follow his lead). I suspect this could in fact go either way depending on the abilities of the individual partners.

I believe that the ideal situation, for people, is to have sex to have babies only; but only after marriage. And in addition if you are not able to control yourself and your need, then get married and each of the helpers should then help each other over this need.

The worst thing possible is to go looking for someone to help you outside of marriage. No good comes from this source.

Let's take an aside here and talk about idols. God early on in the Bible tells us to have no idols before us. We have a hard time as human being following orders. We have idols before us all the time. Money is probably the foremost of the possible idols. Many of us worship money and the power and the prestige it can bring. Some actually worship money itself. Other items of worship can be sports, TV, children, beauty, golf, alcohol, drugs, flowers, robots; anything can be an idol to us. The Bible shows us once God sent a bronze serpent to save the Israeli people during their wanderings, from poison snakes; they ended up worshipping it until God had it destroyed. We ourselves can be an idol. God should be our god and no other things, no good can come from anything else, for God is the source of all that is good.

As I opined earlier, most of us need a helper, not just for having children and sex but to keep us grounded and honest. Too often people who are too alone or too closed to other people go off on tangents to reality. They get lost. Being broken is bad enough but to be lost and broken makes it even more difficult to recover to functionality. I think it is similar to what our ministers once talked about, in that, people who miss church for a long period of time are like a boat normally tied to a pier, if it is left untied it just drifts further and further away from the point of stability (the church). Maybe people are like that if they don't have a "pier" to tie to, any way thanks to my wife for being my point of stability.

Thought I would add a blurb here about close relationships and the changes we go through when we form them. All I can do is tell how I feel. After Sue and I were married for a lot of years I could feel that my natural defenses were dropped and I could share without fear of being hurt. Sue tells me that this is just me and not everyone has these defenses in place. She says that the defenses she always assumed were from my childhood. I just thought everyone had them in place except when a long term relationship allowed them to be able to be dropped. I do know once you (or maybe just me) drop them if the other person in the relationship causes you hurt, it goes very deeply and can cause an anger response (not violence but a hurtful anger).

I have always noted a distinct difference in male and female humor (far beyond the Venus/Mars thing – more like we are not in the same solar system). This humor, either type, when it is not understood as humor, can impact as hurt. I feel bad for the many times I probably hurt someone, especially my wife Sue, when I only thought I was being funny.

Ephesians not only has a great guideline (help) for our marriages but also for raising our children and running our families. I found this out too late for my life but not for yours. Check it out.

CHAPTER 13: TESTIMONIES

John 5:31 "If I testify about myself, my testimony is not valid. There is another who testifies in my favor, and I know that his testimony about me is valid. You have sent to John and he has testified to the truth. Not that I accept human testimony; but I mention it (so) that you may be saved."

This is a statement by Jesus and the John mentioned was John the Baptist but I think, including a number of testimonies by good people may serve somewhat the same purpose: witness that Jesus Christ is Lord - so that you may be saved.

I thought a sampling of a number of people I have met with compelling testimonies would be a good addition to this book. Testimonies are a favorite example of mine, of how our Lord works in our lives even today. These examples are widely varied and I find all inspirational. I have read dozens, if not hundreds, of testimonies. They are also an excellent way for us to review our lives and see how our walks to sanctification are progressing (or not). I would really highly suggest for you to pray and sit down and begin writing yours as soon as possible. And then review and edit them every few years. You may see some reflections of yourself in the attached examples (remember they are directed by the same hand that has interwoven everything else in the universe) since God many times uses beautiful patterns over and over again.

BOB FILLER: this is how I came to have faith and trust in our Lord Jesus Christ. When I was a child, my mother took me to Sunday school at a Presbyterian church. As I became a teenager, I decided church was not for me. I lived apart from God, no church, no Bible. I developed a drinking problem, which turned into an addiction. As I approached 40 years old, the addiction became uncontrollable. I was afraid that I was going to harm myself or someone else because of it.

I turned to God and prayed sincerely for 2 things: that he would help me control my drinking and that he would help me find a woman who I could trust and one that would trust me. I prayed this for a few weeks and I met a woman at a going away party. We went out to a nightclub the following weekend. As usual I had too much to drink and on the drive home I was arrested for a DUI and because of where I work I had to report it. I was sent to a Rehab and part of that was to attend AA meetings. At the last required AA meeting, as we went around the room and spoke about our problems, a man stood up and said: "I'm a follower of Jesus Christ and if you want to be free from your addiction, invite Jesus Christ into your life and ask him to take away your addiction and he will I guarantee it, because he did it for me. Then he gave simple instructions: when your leave here, go home, go to your room, shut the door, get on your knees and ask Jesus Christ, no beg him, to come into your life. Admit you are a sinner and admit as many sins as you can think of, ask him to be your savior and ask him to take away your addiction. Then he gave a short gospel message about Christ's love, his forgiveness of sins and his promise of everlasting life."

This message was so powerful to me, that when I got home, I did exactly what he said and I poured out my heart to Christ and I invited him into my life.

As time went by, I began to notice a change in my attitude, my thoughts, the way I interacted with people and my view of the world. For instance, if I would get a crude joke in my e-mail, it wasn't funny anymore. I would send it back and ask them not to send me anything like that. Other people also saw the change in me. One fellow asked me if I became a Christian, and I only shrugged my shoulders because I didn't know.

As more time went by, I felt compelled to find a church, and I believe I was led to First Presbyterian Church in Beaver. As I began to listen to the sermons and joined a Bible study, I saw that the change I was going through was normal for a Christian. Christ and the Holy Spirit were changing me. You see, it wasn't something I read about, it wasn't something I decided to do. It just happened to me. That is the foundation of my faith. Christ is real in my life, because of the change that occurred in me through Him.

That simple prayer when I first turned to God and asked Him to help me control my drinking was answered. I have been sober for over 10 years without any more rehab or AA meetings. Just as that man guaranteed, I believe Christ removed that addiction. The other part of the prayer: the woman that I was with the night of my arrest became my wife exactly 2 years later. God blessed our marriage, beyond any expectation I had. I could not have picked a better woman than Debbie. We believe that God's hand was in our meeting and our marriage.

I give thanks to Christ each and every day for answering my prayer so powerfully and for coming into my life, changing me, and saving me from my addictive self.

Testamony of Don Collings: *I had the blessing of being raised in a Christian household. From the time I was an infant I was brought to church by my parents. About the time I was 11 years old I began to understand that I could not rely on my parent's faith for salvation. At a Sunday evening service, the Holy Spirit convicted me of my own sin and my need for Christ. I understood that Jesus had died to pay the cost of my sins and had made the way for me to become part of God's family. Later that night in my room I called out to God and received His merciful gift of salvation.*

I continued to grow throughout grade school and most of high school, but had a pretty serious time of rebellion in college. Looking back on those years I can clearly see that though at times I may have tried to abandon the Lord, He was always faithful to me and never let me go. One example of His unbelievable grace during my time of rebellion is that He allowed me to meet my future wife, Mary.

As I became first a husband and then a father, God continued to draw me closer to Himself as I realized my complete inadequacy to lead a family. It was during those early years of our marriage that I more fully devoted myself to Jesus. I continue to fail God very often, but I can see myself steadily growing in His grace year after year.

Over the years the Lord has provided many opportunities for me to grow through His Word, including calling me to be the Teaching Director of the Community Bible Study in Beaver for the past 10 years. I am very thankful to the Lord, that two years ago He brought us to First Presbyterian Church where His Name is honored and His Scripture is taught faithfully.

MARY COLLINGS TESTIMONY: I am the 2nd oldest of 10 kids. We were regular church goers. I considered myself religious. I had no doubts – I was going to heaven. My identity was wrapped up in believing that I was a good person.

Fast forward to college – I meet Don who was a born again Christian. He asked me, "If you were to stand before God today and He were to say, "Mary why should I let you into My heaven" what would you say?"

I answered, "God, I've done a lot of good things. Basically I'm a good person. I've done some bad stuff, but I know that my good outweighs my bad." I believed that God would weigh my good deeds against my bad and that I would not have a problem getting into heaven.

I think that Don probably cringed, but we remained close. At this time, one of my younger sister's was really sick. Theresa was born with congenital heart defects. She had a number of surgeries, but the doctors were unable to repair her heart enough. She died just before Christmas of my junior year of college. She was 3 and half.

I went through a period of profound sadness. Don was in ROTC at the time. After morning exercise or drill, he would knock on my door and tell me to get to class. If he hadn't done this I probably wouldn't have made it to class most days.

Senior year progressed and I was slowly coming out of my depression. Don and I were growing closer. We recognized that we had different beliefs about God. My God was an impersonal score keeper. His was personal, and active in his life and much more that I didn't understand.

Don suggested that we read the Bible and talk about it. At this point we had just graduated and lived 5 hours apart. I readily agreed, fully convinced that he would come around to my way of thinking about God and religion.

We began in the Book of James. I began to see God as good and holy in a way that I never had. I started to have doubts about the worth of my "good deeds". I could see that my definition of God fell far short of God's goodness. In Romans 3:23 it says, "We all have sinned and fall short of the glory of God" this is what I was beginning to understand.

Next we read the Gospel of John.

(Note) When I met Don, he told me that he was born again. This cracked me up because my only exposure to people who were "born again" was our cleaning lady who said, "praise the Lord" all of the time and a church group that stayed at my parents summer camp, who shouted and waved their hands in the air hollering "Amen" etc. I was struck by how nice and normal Don was. He did not fit my stereotype for "born again".

We got to John chapter 3 where Jesus and Nicodemus are talking.

This was a light bulb moment for me. The Holy Spirit enabled me to understand this passage as I never had before. I realized that God was working in my life and I too was being "born again". I recognized that my deeds weren't good and that I could not earn heaven. I now knew that I didn't just do "bad stuff", I was a sinner.

Romans 6:23 says, "For wages of sin is death, but the gift of God is eternal life in Christ Jesus our Lord." God showed me that Jesus, who had never sinned, had died on the cross, and was punished for my sins, so that I might be forgiven.

I called Don on the phone and said, "I'm born again." He was confused at first and then amazed at how God works. It still cracks me up that God used that passage about being "born again" to open my eyes to His truth. I had held such a mistaken view about what born again actually meant, but now I got it.

In 2nd Corinthians it says" everyone who is in Christ is a new creation, the old is gone the new has come". Right away I noticed some changes in my life. I had previously had a strong belief in luck. Almost immediately, I recognized that if something went well I needed to thank God for it. I began to realize that He was working in my life, blessing me. I realized that there was no such thing as luck.

Very soon after I was saved, the Lord gave me a tremendous gift. After my sister died, I was sad for a long time. During that time and after, I couldn't remember her very well. I lost specific memories of the cute little things she did. Over a period of a few weeks, He restored my memories of my sister.

If I was asked that same question that Don asked me all those years ago, "If you were to stand before God and He asked you why He should let you into Heaven?" My answer would be quite different. I would say something like, "Lord, I am a sinner. There is nothing that I can do to make up for my offense. You are rich in mercy. (What)

Jesus did on the cross (is what is needed) to forgive the sin of your children. It is not because of what I have done, but because of what you have done that will get me into heaven".

Testimony of Peg Buck: *Before receiving Christ as my Lord, I was very independent and focused on works, and achievement. I always knew about Jesus and accepted Him as my Savior. I joined our church when I was 13. When I went blind in the summer of 1996, I realized I needed help that only God could give me. I had to trust and depend on Him and not on my job and career successes, or even other people.*

I was totally helpless without Him. People were not the answer. Only God could get me back on the path where I belonged.

When I realized that I had been focusing my time and efforts on the wrong things in life, I repented, asked God to forgive me and take my life and use it for his purposes. Christ forgave me and started bringing me out of the pit I was in. The Holy Spirit taught me and I began to grow in Him more and more each day.

I redirected my attention on the Lord, left my career and the people who hindered my growth with God, and focused on God, His work and prayer and worship. I trusted Him, based on His promises in the Bible, to meet all of my needs and He did.

My eyes were healed. He taught me how to live debt free. I walk with Him and He gives me peace in every area of my life.

Jim Buck Testimony (note here I edited this testimony since it was on tape – advised Jim he should be the one writing a book)

It's been a long preparation time for me, to reach this point. I'm JB, and JA (Jeff Arnold) asked JB to talk about JC (Jesus Christ).

You know how Jeff works, he asked me to give this testimony and there is no way I can do it. But JC wants me to do it, so you won't see me; you'll see JC working in me. I'm not a speaker or a preacher but I am a talker. So here goes. Have you seen cartoons with a little angel/Jesus on a shoulder and a devil on the other shoulder? That's me. When I'm driving in car, I look to Jesus as I'm driving or waiting in a grocery line many times. Well, one day, I was leaving a grocery store and I thought should I go home? Jesus said you've got some time to visit some elderly people in a nursing home, and the devil said no, go home the ball game is on. But I did go to the nursing home, that day and I felt so much better to take this path, giving care to others.

Recently, after listening to another testimony (by a church member) and I so much identified with his testimony (even though I'm much older). I told Jeff how much I liked the testimony and that's how I got here today. I was raised a Christian but just lacked something, some doubt in my life. I think what I needed to get to is faith. Faith is what brought me to where I'm at. Jeff has talked about plateaus of faith, and how you can grow your faith. I told him my faith is now where Jesus is, here with me, he is my strength, my courage, and he got me up here today (in front of the congregation).

Prayer, a lot of us pray, at dinner, at church, but some don't pray daily. Norman Vincent Peale said we should pray at least 15 minutes a day. I get up in the morning and Jesus' picture is on the wall by my bed, and I thought I was home alone, but I was not alone, Jesus was there with me. I thought I was alone for 54 years but I wasn't. Jesus is with me all the time. I became aware of Jesus, 12 years ago. But getting back to the praying part, a lot of this may not be relative to your life, for some of us just go to Jesus when we're in trouble. We put Him away when we don't need him.

In the Army, I flew to Illinois from Texas and the airplane's motor leaked oil. We then had to make an emergency landing in Ogden Utah. It was a foggy morning, at a backward town. Radar was old fashioned. We missed the landing 2 or 3 times but finally landed, but missed the runway. Another time I was stationed in Korea and had R&R in Japan. On another plane, the plane circled Mt. Fuji a number of times (so I knew something was wrong). Someone came back and said the landing gear was stuck, and they were going to try to pump it down but were not sure if it would hold. Well down we went into Crishini Airbase in Japan. Fire trucks and emergency vehicles were on the runway. I prayed a lot because I was in trouble. Those are faith builders, my faith definitely improved after that.

Then my son Jeffrey got hit by a car in 1986, he got hurt real bad. His heart stopped 2 times. My wife and I and prayed a lot, at St. Vincent's Health Center in Erie Pennsylvania. We really, really prayed God would save Jeff's life. This was the first plateau of faith I got to. I thought Jim would take care of him, but please God save him. God did save him and he was healed and is now a baker at Kretchmar's (bakery) where I visit a lot. My next faith demanding situation is my wife's death in 1990 and it really took a lot out of me. She took her own life but God got me through it and Jesus really entered my body, and my life, and my soul. My whole life changed and I gave it to

Christ. First, as a deacon, then in other works. I would go to retirement homes, nursing homes, rehab centers and visit elderly everywhere and by doing so Christ just kept building me up so much. I could just see Christ continuing working in me and I just want to be his helper.

I would like to tell you a story, a true story, about a member of our church and an elder. He was so involved in our church and was moved to a nursing home in Beaver County and he had Alzheimer's. He many times was found dressed up in suits waiting for church. So they had to explain it was not time. He got worse and worse till he didn't recognize anyone. So I was visiting him one day plus another person there. So I went up to see this former elder and found he couldn't talk and just was sitting there with a card (birthday) on his tray, just staring at it. So I thought I would help and read him the card, so I did. So I thought I would leave and told the old guy I would see him in a couple of days (because I used to visit this home every couple of days). I got to the door and thought I would pray with the old guy. I took his hand in mine and began praying, after about 30 seconds I finished and began to walk away. I got to the door and heard as clear as a bell the old guy say out loud - "thanks Jim".

Don't know if any of you have ever been around these type patients but to hear him say this to me this was one of the greatest rewards I could ever get and I'm still not sure where it came from but "thanks Jim" will always stick with me.

I would like to read something to you – Psalm 34:4 I sought the Lord, and he heard me; he delivered me from all my fears. He absolutely will always. Just look where he has me today. He is the only unchanging factor in the world today.

Seek the Lord; it may be enough to just spend 15 minutes a day with our Lord.

I wrote this prayer: Dear Lord, this a thank you note to God. This is Jim, trusting in you and my best friend Jesus. I hope you will give me the words, the opportunity, the courage to reach out to people here today and that something I shared here with all these people will in some way help someone. Be with us, Lord, the rest of our lives and with us forever and ever.

Thank you, Lord, for our church, our leaders, and thank you for each other. Amen

TESTIMONY OF VIC SIHA: *This is my testimony, of what the Lord has done in my life. I was raised by Christian parents in the Coptic*

*Orthodox Church (church founded by Mark in Alexandria Egypt.)
I was surrounded by all the trappings of Christianity, but I had no clue
of the essence of who Jesus Christ was. At the age of 17 my conversion
occurred. When I first heard and understood what the great news of
the greatest exchange in the history of mankind. That, first I was a
sinner destined for eternal wrath, and that He paid for all my sins, and
that I was freed from the penalty of my sins. Years later, as the Lord
blessed us with "eyes that could see, and ears that could hear," I finally
understood that He also freed us from the bondage of sinning. The
more I study the Holy Scriptures, the bigger and bigger His grace is
to me and my own unworthiness looms in an overwhelming fashion.
Now, I can see and perceive His hand of mercy and love from the very
beginning leading me; convicting, chastening and filling me with His
presence. It truly is amazing what He can do! By His grace, I fully
understand the doctrines of grace in depth, from my total depravity
to His promises of preservation (and perseverance) of His adopted
children. All to the praise of His majesty and glory.*

TESTIMONY OF DAVE MATEER: I grew up in a stable Christian home
under the care of very wise and loving parents. Our family went
to Sunday school and church every Sunday, but my parents never
pushed me to "make a decision" for Christ. In ninth grade, during
our church's confirmation class to join the church, I first heard the
gospel starting from creation, the fall, and redemption, and made a
profession of faith.

Looking back on that event, I now recognize that I was the classic
false convert, eager for an escape from eternal punishment but
lacking repentance and submission to the lordship of my Savior. I was
a hypocrite living in two worlds: among my "spiritual" friends and
church family, I was the well-behaved, respectful "good boy". At the
same time, I was enjoying the rebellions of youth with my heathen
friends. I conformed my behavior to earn the approval of men, in
whatever crowd I happened to find myself.

Just after graduation from high school, I did something very
selfish that caused great pain to a friend. Rather than excusing my
sin, this friend called me on it and held me accountable. The Lord
used that circumstance to grant genuine repentance. I understood
that it was my sin (not merely an abstract sin of humankind) that
needed to be atoned for on the cross. I believe it was at this point
in my life (although I have no exact date) that God gave me new

life through faith in the perfect obedience and atoning sacrifice of his Son.

Since then, God has given me an increasing desire to know His Word and live for His Kingdom. Although my walk has often not been as consistent as I would like, I am grateful for His guidance through His Spirit and inexhaustible patience.

Testimony of Diane Mateer: *When I was 6 years old, I realized that if I died that night, I would go to hell. I was very upset about this and spoke to my mother at length about it that night. Later that same month, the pastor came out and talked with me as well and at that time, I believed in Jesus as the one who died in my place and for my sins. I would say that I got saved at that time, but my walk with the Lord has been a journey over many years since I was that small child who professed belief.*

When I was between 7 and 8 years of age, I was baptized and then when I was between 9 and 10 years of age, I felt a strong call to the mission field. Since that time, the Lord has graciously led me and guided me along His path. I know there were times that I was either not walking as closely with the Lord as I should have been, or times when I was very self-righteous in my faith, and yet God graciously has continued to draw my heart close to His. He has been abundantly gracious and kind to me as He has led me on this path, and for that I am forever grateful.

When I was 20 years old, I was accepted to the Rod Box Mission Program at Grove City College. This was a wonderful experience for me and I was able to live and work in Russia for 2 months between my junior and senior years of college. The Lord graciously grew me a lot that summer and solidified my desire to serve Him in missions in some capacity. It was not long after that experience that Dave (husband) and I started dating and two years after we started dating, we got married. Through marriage, the Lord showed me what a selfish person I was and then when we started having children, I realized I was the most selfish person in the world. Yet, still the Lord was working in my heart and drawing me to Himself. I suppose having our first 4 children in less than 6 years was a bit of a trial of faith for me. I had a crisis within myself and wondered if I was even saved. Even through that, the Lord was drawing me. He wanted to remind me that anything good is from Him and any ability I have-down to the smallest thing in parenting or life – is from Him and not from me.

After Dave and I had been married for almost 10 years, we felt called to go into missions together. We applied and were accepted with New Tribes Mission. In 2008, we went to work and lived at NTM headquarters based in Florida. In working for New Tribes, the Lord took away everything that we depended on – Dave's job, insurance, our house, our friends, and our church family; that we had known and then cast us onto Himself. In casting us upon Himself, we found Him to be very faithful, dealing gently with those whom He had called.

Now that we are in a new phase in our lives, I am anxious to see what the Lord has in store for us next. What lessons, good things, and knowledge of Christ only the Lord knows, but I pray I ever grow closer to Him on the journey.

TESTIMONY OF BILL CUTRI: I was raised Presbyterian in a Christian home although my family did not attend church on a regular basis. I was invited to attend Sunday school by a grade school class mate in 3rd grade. Vanport Presbyterian Church had a small congregation and was within walking distance of my home. Reverend Bell was the first of two pastors named Bell that would shape my Christian life. Sometime, in those grade school years, I accepted Jesus Christ as my personal savior. I attended Sunday school through high school and served as president of the Junior High and then Senior High Youth Fellowships. Although I was attending a reformed Presbyterian college, Geneva, I only attended church on an intermittent basis and when I did go to church it was at First Presbyterian Church of Beaver, where my parents were members. In my senior year of college, I started dating a high school class mate and she invited me to go to church with her on Sunday morning and Wednesday nights at the First Presbyterian Church of Rochester. Later I would be the luckiest man on earth as I married that great Christian woman in the same church.

During the spring of 1972, a Billy Graham Crusade, came to Rochester High School. There, another Reverend Bell changed how I was leading my life. Through his preaching, I came to the realization that I could not share the throne with God. He had to be the King of my life and only He could sit on the throne. I had to step off the throne, bow down and acknowledge that he was sovereign over all of my life. On that day, I rededicated my life to Jesus Christ. The next major step that happened in my Christian growth was in the area of tithing. After much prayer, my wife and I decided we would try tithing our paycheck. I found out what a great joy it is to be able to happily support Christian endeavors with the money we set aside in a separate checking account that was the Lord's. God has blessed me in so many other ways as I have continued to walk with Him as my Lord and Savior.

TESTIMONY OF JOYE HAGEN: *I was raised by a loving mom and dad, along with all four of my grandparents. My mom and her parents were my examples of Christianity in our family. My mom took my brother, sister, and I to Sunday school and church every week. She encouraged us to join in church activities and to be involved in service where ever and whenever we could. I was living a Christian life or at least I thought I was.*

I first asked Jesus into my heart when I was 9 or 10 years old. And I say first, because at the time I knew I wanted to be a Christian and to be a good person but I didn't really understand what Jesus had done for me. I don't know if anyone ever told me or if my heart just wasn't ready to hear, but it all changed one summer.

It wasn't until I was 16 years old that I really understood what Christ had done on the cross and what he wanted from me. I went to a conference with my youth group and thousands of other teenagers. It was within the first night's meeting that I gained an insight and a new understanding of Jesus and the relationship he wanted to have with me. Because that's what it is a two-way relationship. He doesn't just want me to be a "good" person. He wants to be that shoulder I cry on when I'm sad, that friend to laugh with when I'm on top of the world and the one I share my most secret fears with. Because once I have that relationship, that trust and faith in him, then he can guide me through my roughest times and most importantly my happiest times. Because it wasn't until I saw His big picture that I understood it's normal to lean on Jesus when we're sad and hurt, we all do it. But we have a lot of moments when we put Jesus on a shelf until the next big problem comes up.

It's something I have to ask Jesus to help me with every day. I have to ask Him to be in my heart to remind me to see Him in everything and to glorify Him in the littlest things I do every day of my life.

We don't always have big problems to run to God with but we always have our day to day routine where God can use us to shine for Him and spread His love.

Philippians 4:13 "I can do everything through Him who gives me strength."

It doesn't say I can do the big things or the scary things but EVERYTHING!

Proverbs 3:5-6 Trust in the Lord with all your heart and lean not on your own understanding in all your ways acknowledge Him, and He will make your paths straight.

THE FOLLOWING IS THE TESTIMONY OF MY DAUGHTER ANGELA: I woke up. My eyes were still closed, but I was awake. The taste of stale smoke and Jack Daniels lingered on my breath, as I laid there trying to recall the nights' events and figure out where I was exactly. I thought about the night before, spent like many I had experienced over the past five years of college, filled with drinking, dancing, and an occasional illegal substance. Embarrassed, I opened my eyes to find a guy that I barely knew, looking into mine. Thank god nothing sexual had happened- he had not taken advantage of my vulnerability. Little did I know, that God uses all things, and He was there with us, and that my eyes were about to be really "opened".

I was raised in a home that believed in the concept of God and Jesus, but we were not followers of Him. Church was an activity reserved for holidays. Now, as I reflect on my childhood, I recognize the people that were placed in my life to tell me about a savior named Jesus. He was there, protecting me, molding me, using all of the worldly stuff for His greater good. Depending on my age, I received this news with various attitudes. During college, I pitied those that were not involved in the party/social scene. Whenever I saw organizations such as Campus Crusaders, I fled, rolling my eyes at the freaks. By that fateful morning, however, I was growing tired of my lifestyle. I was three months shy of graduating as a nurse. I was realizing that it was not fulfilling, I felt so empty. That morning that I woke up in a strange place, I was looking into the eyes of my future husband. I certainly had not planned on a relationship, especially with someone younger. I had just ended a long term relationship, and I was ready to move on to post college life. God had a plan, though, and after many ups and downs, we were married three years later.

Dave was raised in a Christian home, always knowing Jesus as his Lord and Savior. His family received me with open arms, patiently answering any questions I had about Christianity, loving me and all of my faults, and witnessing to me in a way that I received. During the periods that Dave and I would have a break in our relationship,

God would always provide someone to take their place and witness to me. He protected me in times that I would turn away, but I always thought about Him. We were living in Florida, attending a Pentecostal church with his sister and her family. Even though we were "living in sin", Dave's parents did not reject us, but loved us. We were both starting to feel convicted that our choice was not a good one, so we were going to marry. Our wedding was to be held on the beach, but this upset Dave's mom. For some reason, my usual rebellious self relinquished, and we agreed to get married by Dave's sister's pastor. This required premarital counseling, and regular church attendance. The music, praise and worship, and pastor were used by God to speak to my soul. It was as if a thirst that I had was quenched. The answer to my seeking was Jesus- I accepted Him as my Lord and Savior, asking Him to live in my heart in October 1997.

Fast forward to June 2008, eleven years, two little boys, an up and down Christian walk, later. We had finally found a church home after searching for many years. I was a member of an organization called MOPS. I remember going the first day, not knowing anyone, feeling as if I was being pulled in- I felt like running, scared of rejection, but I actually followed through and joined, becoming actively involved. The church which hosted our MOPS was a Church of the Nazarene. We tried it out, and felt like we belonged. We had been seeking a church home for seven years! I was driving home from Pittsburgh, taking the Breezewood exit off of the Pennsylvania turnpike. As I drove down the mountain, tears filled my eyes. I had called my 3 year old sons pediatrician, requesting blood work for what I knew was going to be cancer. I just knew, as an RN, as a mom, I knew my boy was very sick. Dave and my parents doubted the seriousness of what I thought was happening. We were driving home to Baltimore, where I knew waited some heartbreaking news and a long road. I looked over the valley as we descended into it, off of the mountaintop. I heard a voice that said, "You have to pick a side now". I understood this voice, and who was saying it. For too long, I did not take my faith seriously. I straddled the fence, claiming that my heart and soul belonged to my Lord, but my actions did not reflect this internal relationship. I still did things that I knew were not alright, and I would pray for forgiveness, but always holding a few things back. Things that I thought I could not live without, essentials to life. However, I realized in that moment, when God instructed me to pick, I had to commit, really, fully commit my heart to Him. I was headed into a valley, both literally and figuratively, and my choice was to do it with Him. I reflected back on the years leading up to 2008, and was awestruck by the preparation of God for what He knew was going to happen. He had provided us with a church family, my MOPS sisters, neighbors that we had recently met, and many, many other things-too many to name. We actually felt at peace, because God knew my son was going to have leukemia, his eventual diagnosis. He allowed it to happen, prepared us, and would continue to be by our side through the experience. Never once did He leave us- nor will He. We have lived out that "all things" work for the glory of God. I continue to grow and to mess up and grow again every single day. I keep seeking Him daily, chasing Him, because I know, for absolute sure, that no drug, no person, no purchase, no vacation-nothing that this world has to offer will fill me up. He is the only answer. He is who we are all seeking, even though most of us don't realize it. He is right there, waiting to be sought and chased, with open arms for us when we are ready to enter them.

Chapter 14: Dreams that I Remember

The oldest dream I can remember, that impacted me, was when I was very young. I don't remember how old I was, but I was in a movie theater. There were a lot of other kids there behaving badly. I remember thinking I would leave early and steal a bicycle that someone may have parked outside the theater. I remember an old fellow behind me read my mind, and said not to do this, but to go on in my life and be a good person. I did as I was told and that's the end of that dream. Not much, huh? But for some reason it really affected me.

The next dream that I can remember was lying in bed one morning after I was married, I remember the sun impacting my closed eyelids and that triggered a math progression and that was absolutely amazing, and it involved tangents of the light path and the earth's seasonal tilt. The speed of the earth's rotation and many other inputs I will never be able to repeat or even follow, but the end result of the computation was it is 7:05 EDT. I was going to be late for work!!!! I jumped out of bed, (it was 7:05) dressed, and rushed out of the house and got to work just in time.

The vision of what I needed to do in my life was that of a hand written letter, with many items on it with the first two items: go to church and read the bible. I have already communicated how that affected my life so I won't repeat it except the number 3 item on the list was to stop spending so much of our money on vacations. Now let me state that we had just booked a cruise to Alaska, and paid for it; so I just naturally thought God did not mean this vacation. From the time we got to

Seattle, and for several weeks after our return, I could not hear, my ears were plugged up solid (inside and both ears). The most miserable experience I've ever had. What I learned from this was, I did not listen and was rewarded with loss of hearing. Not sure if this is what others think, but it is what I took away from this event.

About a year later, I had another dream that I will always remember. My wife and I were walking in a strange place and there were some monks tending olive trees (biggest olives I have ever seen – big as apples) they told us not to eat the olives but Sue picked one up and bit into it and instantly fell down. I carried her to the mountain area where the monks lived. Next, Sue was back awake, we went through a canyon (very skinny) and as we came out of the canyon (kind of like coming out of the tunnel into Pittsburgh) we viewed an absolutely beautiful ancient town. A very large man, named Bear, came up to us and took us on a tour of the village/town. I left Sue taking a nap, and when I returned she had become a very old wrinkled person. Bear told me the only way I could save her was by finding a very rare alpine flower up on the mountains. I went and found it and returned and saved her.

About a year after the last dream, I had an even wilder dream. Sue and I were traveling in a car (Sue was driving as normal). We went over a mountain road and it ended and we flew off the mountain and crashed (blackness then) the next event was awakening in a small room with a lot of people dressed in white, standing in line to get to a desk manned by other people in white. Off to the side was a table of hot cherry pie ala mode. Nobody said anything so I went to the table with the pie and began eating (it was hot so you just can't wait – the ice cream will melt). When I finished I turned around and everyone was gone; the workers, the line, and even Sue. And down I went back to earth, awakening again in a hospital bed, with the knowledge I had work to do here on earth. This is where I got the Angels In Training idea (first name for Carpenter's CHORE). Not sure, but I had the feeling that everyone took either an elevator or an escalator (up I presume and hope).

That's it for dreams, not sure what they all mean but I really feel they are important to me and I'm stuck with them. Why don't you write yours down and think about them.

CHAPTER 15: LOOKING BACK

I think my grandmother having me pulling weeds at her house and me being obsessed with (weeds) decades later may not be just an accident. I am the seed they planted. I just thank my Lord and Savior for providing the help I needed to begin and continue my life with Him. I look forward to once again seeing my grandparents in a few years and just loving them.

Let me explain: my grandmother Malone and my grandmother Edna both had experiences I was told about. Both had their hearts stop and were medically resuscitated. Both were distraught that they were brought back from a wonderful place with loved ones. I will always keep this in mind. A minister of the church we go to in Florida closed a eulogy one time with Ephesians 3:18, stating that the deceased person, only now was able to fully grasp the width, and length, and height, and depth of the love of Christ. This is indeed my hope.

One thing I'd like to say right here, when I'm gone please don't mourn for me. My life has been all I could ever ask for and much more than I deserve. Really know I'm not "done" and will still be around but with my Lord and Savior. I'm sure He has work for me to do, to help me out in eternity. To my kids: no I'm not sick and don't plan on dying soon but when I do, this all pertains.

A thought after looking back: isn't it sad that our God had to come down to earth to show us how to walk. And always remember planting seeds require an action.

Looking back on all I have written I can see one consistent theme: God has been watching over me for my entire life. He has helped me through each step of my walk, he has put doors to open, and people to guide and walk with me. I praise and thank him for his help, and this just goes to prove: **Everybody Needs Help.**

A POEM

ALONE

Dead and dying on no where's path
Just forlorn mistakes of mother's math
Afraid or pathetically stupid-smart
Away from those lanes of vacuum depart.

Tomorrow's dawn shall not deliver
Your bodies nor souls from that river
That river you call your life,
which begins nowhere and ends in strife

and then
WITH GOD

Now God is patient and oh so merciful
My arrogance tested both - I'm such a fool!
God led me with his wondrous handiwork
And showed me how I was really a jerk.

Studying the world and all of nature
I got caught up in complete rapture.
And finally I realized all this was created,
A creator exists, and my future is fated.

I prayed to Him and asked what can I do?
Instantly He showed me "Nothing - I did it for you"
We only need to accept His love and follow Him,
Life any other way is really hopeless and grim

I learned in time, in scripture and spirit
God's love is wondrous and we should never fear it.

Salvation is neither by goodness nor lot.
but given freely by what Jesus wrought

What now must I do with this bounty of love?
From the One I adore - that One up above.
Give it to all who like me need ways to mend,
Cause I know now my Lord's supply is without end.

THE VEIL

The world through the veil is an unknown reality,
we cannot know, with our limited mentality

We try …. And try …. And though we stare,
True vision comes only through prayer.

The unknown shapes move & jump - the cloth so thinly sliced,
But for us focus and truth are only possible through Christ.

His wondrous word will set us free --- to see
My God --- He is Holy, Holy, Holy!

There are so many people I would like to thank for their guidance over the years but I would never be able to list them all but every single one has this in common – they are God loving people. Foremost among them are my ministers Jeff, Henry, Marc, and Don.

CHAPTER 16: HOPE

Every day during my daily prayers, I spend some time praying for comfort, peace, and hope for a number of people who I think need God's help to get through a tough period. A couple of years ago as I was praying I could only remember 2 of these things and I had lost one of the words (another getting older thing I guess). This forgetting worried me off and on all day. The next day as I was praying the word came back and I felt so much relief. I had just gone for a whole day with no HOPE! And it was not a pleasant feeling.

This event, though seemingly minor, got me to thinking of the absolute necessity of having hope, and how horrible it must be to have no hope in actuality.

As a follower of Jesus Christ, God is my hope continually and the Holy Spirit dwells within me and reassures me. Before I was a Christian, my youth, and other things, filled this void to some extent, but as the years moved on the vacancy was apparent and worry filled the space.

From the dictionary: hope - a desire accompanied by expectation of or belief in fulfillment or to expect with desire.

A lot is taught to us about hope in the Bible:

Psalm 42:5, Psalm 62:5, Proverbs 13:12, Isaiah 40:31, Romans 5:5, Romans 8:24, Romans 12:12, Romans 15:4, Colossians 1:27, 1John 3:3, 1Thessalonians 5:8, 1Timothy 6:17, Titus 2:13, Hebrews 6:19, and Hebrews 11:1 are just a few sources.

With all the above in mind, our hope is in our Lord and to be in His presence. During Bible study last year, God's reaffirming guidance, through a brother, was that our prayers should be directed much more towards achieving God's presence than His provisions (worldly concerns and needs). Prayer and knowing God (Christ) has given us the Holy Spirit as a deposit, guaranteeing what is to come. He is our Hope.

Thinking more about the tragedy of not having hope in Christ: there are millions of people out there that have huge vacancies in their lives. These holes undoubtedly leave them hungering for what they are missing or being filled with other things like drugs, alcohol, immoralities, worshipping idols (money, possessions, etc.).

There are those who hope for a future with a god because of their individual actions in this world, whether good, kind, or evil and violent. Their Hope is based on their actions and thus not to be relied on. Our Hope is one of faith on a salvation guaranteed by a faithful and righteous God who has freely given this, by His grace, is present within us to reassure us, and has provided us a Scripture to show us. How great you are Lord.

We should all keep in mind this missing hope that others may have, when we deal with people of the world, and thank our great Rock and Redeemer for providing us with what we would otherwise be missing – HOPE.

After putting together the thoughts on HOPE, I thought it might be good to do the same with Peace, so here goes.

From Webster's New Collegiate Dictionary peace: freedom from civil disturbance or freedom from disquieting or oppressive thoughts or emotions.

A number of advices from the Bible are much more helpful:

Number 6:26, Psalm 34:14, Psalm 119:165, Psalm 122:6, Proverbs 14:30, Proverbs 17:1, Isaiah 9:6, Isaiah 26:3, Isaiah 48:22, Matthew 10:34, Luke 2:14, John 14:27, John 16:33, Romans 5:1, 1 Corintians 7:15, Galatians 5:22, Ephesians 2:14, Philippians 4:7, Colossians 1:20, 1 Thessalonians 5:3, 2 Thessalonians 3:16, 2 Timothy 2:22, 1 Peter 3:11, and Revelations 6:4

Peace we may achieve through God comes by following His Word and being obedient to His Will. Avoid the lures of this world and pursue righteousness.

From all the above it is apparent that Christ is our peace, and only through Him may we have peace in this world. Through Christ we gain all the fruits of the Spirit which include peace. Peace is a desirable condition that should be pursued and valued; and comes only from goodness and love. Never from evil, envy, and hate.

Confusion, Misunderstanding, and/or Stress

In the Bible, Love is mentioned almost 200 times and emphasizes that God loves beyond any doubt.

When confusion, misunderstanding, and/or stress arise as we study the Bible – always keep in mind God's love.

And Remember just TRUST and OBEY. So if you are troubled follow our Lord and trust and obey....however we are also obligated to study and learn as much as we can of our Lord & his Word.

Trust is used about 50 times.

Psalm 71:1 in you O Lord, I put my trust; Let me never be put to shame. Deliver me in your righteousness, and cause me to escape, Incline your ear to me, and save me.

2 Corinthians 3:4 and we have such trust through Christ toward God. Not that we are sufficient of ourselves to think of anything as being from ourselves, but our sufficiency is from God.

Isaiah 26:4 Trust in the Lord forever.

Hebrew 2:13 I will put my trust in Him (God)

Obey is used about 40 times.

Jeremiah 42:6 whether it is pleasing or displeasing, we will obey the voice of the Lord our God.

Acts 5:29 we ought to obey God rather than man.

Hebrews 5:9 and having been perfected, He became the author of eternal salvation to all who obey Him, called by God as High Priest....

Just remember there is always Hope. Even for an old guy like me who was so blind and deaf for 55 years. Just ask for a little help – from our Lord. He will undoubtedly jump right in and help you. Don't forget - we all need a little (or maybe a lot of) pruning. But no matter how much, He can do all things, for He is God.

Bibliography

Books, movies, and radio shows I mentioned or quoted in this publication are:

The Holy Bible, NIV version

Young William P. ,"The Shack", Hackette Book Group, United States, 2009.

Corbett, Steve and Fikkert, Brian; "When Helping Hurts", Moody Publishers,Chicago, 2012.

"It's A Wonderful Life", Frank Capra, 1946, United States, RKO Radio Pictures, Dec. 20, 1946

"The Bickerson's", Philip Rapp, CBS, 1947-1951.

Webster's New Collegiate Dictionary, G&C Merriam Co., United States 1981

Made in the USA
Lexington, KY
06 January 2014